PARDON

The Courage to Be Set Free

Sharon Moman

NEWMAN SPRINGS PUBLISHING
320 Broad Street
Red Bank, NJ 07701

First originally published by Newman Springs Publishing 2021

ISBN 978-1-63692-983-5 (Paperback)
ISBN 978-1-63692-984-2 (Digital)

Printed in the United States of America

To my beloved sons Kenneth, James, and Sean—my heartbeats.

CONTENTS

PREFACE

I was once you, conflicted about whether to stay or leave. This book is not written to decide for you. You, my friend, have already come to a conclusion for yourself based on your own experience. You've already had that talk with yourself. Whether it is staying or leaving, both take tremendous courage. May God be with you during this difficult time as you ponder about your journey that has led you to this point. The road you will choose will no doubt be full of awareness and anxiety. No matter what, remember, God is always with you, and you can always recalibrate at any time.

Exodus

The synonyms of *exodus* are departure, withdrawal, evacuation, leaving, migration, flight, escape, etc. I could write a chapter on each word as it relates to marriage/divorce. During my time of writing this book, I found myself being drawn closer to God. I'd given up my fifteen minutes of daily devotion for an expansive two hours or more study time that also included some motivational speakers on YouTube. It was like I could not get enough. I had been spiritually famished. The more I read or heard God's Word, the more I wanted and needed it. Every sermon checked a box in my soul, and every scripture leaped off the page as if I was reading it for the first time.

Out of all the pain I had gone through from my fleshly fight with man, I bowed my head and thanked God for the consolation prize of my dignity and spiritual awakening. My awaking—new birth, as I like to call it—was May 5. I'll never forget that day and the moment of realization that was occurring. The pain of losing yet another marriage and losing the friendship that I invested in for five years was so intense that all I could do every day, as soon as I called it a day, was to grab something strong to drink to numb the pain. As I tried to sort through all the dysfunction that got us to this point again; my only relief was a bottle of something. This activity, from my recount, occurred for a period of at least ten days before my resurrection. On the morning of April 25, I had to muster the courage to do the unthinkable, file for divorce number 3. Although I knew I had to file because of the potential legal circumstances, I still woke up every day grieving my marriage. It had been almost two weeks since I walked into the county courthouse with documents in hand and my fee of ninety-three dollars in cash when the following occurred in my home later that afternoon.

On May 5, I remember walking past my buffet where all my liquor bottles were stored. I stopped and slowly turned to face the bottles that once held me captive. In that moment, I realized that I was not thirsty for the liquor anymore, nor had I been for the past two days. I cannot explain this aha moment but can only dot down some words on this page. For those of you who have experienced the unimaginable, you know exactly what I'm talking about. For the rest of you, in the words of my grandma; "keep on living." It is only through great pain that you can get an experience like this.

I said to myself, "Oh my god, what is happening?" Normally, I would cry tears of joy, but I didn't have any tears left at that moment. I just lifted my hands in the air. "Only you, Lord, could do this—do this being, soothing my soul from the heart pain I was feeling, and taking away the thirst for the liquor."

I never decided to stop drinking the liquid medicine. I mean, I never said, "Okay, Sharon, next week or next month or in three months, we are going to stop all this drinking." No. I was in too much pain to make any decisions like that. Heck, I just made a life-altering decision of getting a divorce from someone I thought was my friend. Now I've got to give up liquor too? Oh no. That was not me. It was the Lord.

God hears your soul when it cries out. God answers *all* our prayers. We just don't pay attention enough to recognize His answers, which are always the best answers. But every now and then, we do recognize His hand like I did when this occurred. It was at that moment that I also recognized that God had answered another prayer, a prayer for peace. I wanted peace in my dysfunctional life. He gave it to me through the divorce.

I know that doesn't sound Christian, but stay with me for a moment and it will become clear. Not my way but His way, it was during those precious moments of *realization* (another realm) that I repented to God for all my participation in the breakdown of my marriage. I bet you were not expecting that. Yes, it would be very easy to just point fingers at one person in a marriage breakdown and say it is all their fault. But the truth of the matter is, it is both parties' fault. Continue to stay with me here. I know exactly what I did and what I did not do to have a successful marriage this time. Let's begin.

CHAPTER 1

The Call

"Hi, Mrs. Moman. This is the nurse calling from Dr. Brown's office. I'm calling with the results of your Pap." I was not married anymore, so I forgot to hold my breath. In all my marriages, I always held my breath when I received the phone call from the doctor's office for my Pap smear results. Warden (aka husband number 1) put that fear in me. We'll get to that story shortly and why I call my ex-husbands Wardens.

"Your Pap came back abnormal," she said. I sat up straight in the chair. Abnormal, I thought. That's what they say when there are cancer cells present, and I'm in that age range where the percentage of it happening to me were high. It is something in the back of most women's mind always, the C word. I hadn't even given it a second thought that it would be an STD. I had laid that ghost down since we were divorced.

She said, "You have trichomoniasis, and we've called in a prescription at Walgreens for you."

Before I knew it, I was calling him all kinds of four-, five-, and six-letter words. The gentle voice on the other side of the phone was very calm. It was apparent that she had made these calls before and most likely was going to make a few more after she hung up with me. I thanked her for the call, and she advise me to quickly pick up and take all the pills and that everything was going to be okay. I could feel the anger spread through every blood vessel in my body. I said to myself, "He better thank God we're already divorced. As I sat on the bed trying to calm myself down; a part of me was happy to hear the news.

I know that sounds strange, but I knew he had been unfaithful to me, and now I could prove it. I am an evidence-driven person. I will believe everything you tell me until the evidence says otherwise. Although hearing the truth does not soften the blow, it does confirm that women's intuition is real and is not to be discarded ever. In other words, I wasn't crazy when the bad vibes would enter into my spirit when certain female friends of his would call or text. He would always spin it. I just did not have the courage to confront him every single time it happened. I picked which battles I wanted to engage in and left the rest on the table. It was exhausting, and what would I do if during one of the confrontations, I heard the words, "Yes, I'm cheating on you"?

If you confront him and it is confirmed that he has cheated, then what? Are you staying? Are you leaving? If you leave, you must act and act swiftly. Like a lot of women, I had no intentions of acting swiftly. I had become comfortable in my marriage, even in the dysfunction that had settled in. Besides, my mother was dying from cancer. Who had time to deal with a divorce?

As I calmed myself down, I made the call to the Warden. "Hello, Butterfly, it's nice to hear from you. Why are you calling me on the landline instead of my cell?" he said.

I had deleted his numbers. I had to Google search his landline number to make the call. I thought to myself, *Hello my ass*, but I had no intention to show him any more anger. Hurricane Butterfly was a thing of the past. Hurricane Butterfly, as he called me when I was upset, would eventually evolve because his natural instinct was to lie about any and all things. I consider myself to be allergic to people who lie and who are fake. Whenever he would lie in any of our conversations, it usually ended with my yelling and those four-, five-, and six-letter words.

I began the conversation relatively calm. I told him the conversation I had with the nurse and advise him that my call to him was an act of a good citizen and that he should go to his physician to get a prescription. I could have gotten one for him from my doctor's office, but I didn't. The norm is when you've been tested and the results return positive for an STD, you are offered a prescription for yourself and your partner. From the strong language I used while on the phone with the nurse, she was sure, without asking for his name, that I would not give him a script even if she provided me one. I wanted him to take that walk of shame at his doctor's office and at the pharmacy himself.

It angers me that we, as women, are always the ones to hear the news first from the nurse, a stranger on the other end of the phone. Most men, if they are informed that they have an STD, will stop having sex with their partner, accuse the other partner, and/or not tell them for fear of cheating accusations and a breakup. They would rather we take the shame bullet for the team as they wait in the background and lie accordingly.

Of course, he denied ever cheating, so I asked, "Well, how did I get this?"

Not once did he rebut and say you must have cheated and gotten it from someone else. No, not once. Nor did he say, "Butterfly, we've been divorced for the last eight months. Whom have you slept with?" No, the following were just a few excuses—I kid you not— that came forth from his mouth and his evil soul. The first thing he said was that the doctor's office must have gotten the wrong results and for me to call them back to see if they would *retest* me, and he would pay for it.

I replied, "Are you freaking kidding me? These tests are not wrong," I screamed.

I kept saying to myself, *Stay calm, Butterfly. This is how he gets to you.*

He kept repeating that the doctor got it wrong; maybe they mixed up my results with someone else. I said, "So you want me to walk back into my doctor's office and tell them that you said their results are wrong and ask for a retest."

"Yes, Butterfly, and I'll pay for it," he said calmly.

I screamed, "Do you know how low I feel right now from that phone call? And you want me to return to their office for a repeat of this shame I feel and wait a whole week for a phone call of the same."

Then he said, "Maybe you got it from a tub or toilet on one of our trips or something."

Screaming at him again, I yell, "It is called an STD because you can only get it from sexual intercourse. It's not called a BTD for bath transmittal disease or TTD for toilet transmittal disease. It is called STD because it is a sexual transmittal disease."

He kept swearing to God and on his mama's grave repeatedly that he never cheated and that he didn't understand. Still, no words uttered his mouth that it could have been me. He knew better. It wasn't me. It was him. Swearing to God meant nothing to him. He believed more in the universe and the planets than the God who created them, except for when he was in trouble with the law, had to wear an ankle bracelet, and a prison sentence was pending. And based on our conversations over our five years together, he had no respect for his mom. He told everyone he came home to take care of her during her illness. That was a lie. He told me he came home to keep his brother and other relatives from draining her checkbook. Ladies, watch how a man treats or has treated his mom. He will inevitably treat you the same or worse.

After ten minutes of listening to his lies and more conspiracy theories of how I got this STD, I finished the call with, "Get yourself checked out so you don't pass this to anyone else."

His reply was, "Oh, Butterfly, I'm just a hermit since you left. I'm not seeing anybody. I know after this, you'll never come back to me. I'll just spend my days working in my garden and staying in my home."

That sure sounded like an admission to me. But per usual, he was only thinking of himself. *No*, I thought to myself, *you will still be a whoremonger and treat women as transactions like you always do.*

After my conversation with him, I called his cousin, who is a physician. I told him of the situation and begged him to give his cousin a call and listen to reason. "I'm just trying to be a good citizen here," I stated. No matter what he said, somebody is still on his payroll, and no doubt, he already has been in bed with someone since our divorce. I mean, why stop now when you are single. Perhaps it was the ex-girlfriend Cassandra who called him frequently while we were dating and married, or perhaps it was the stranger he took to dinner during his trip to Vegas two weeks after my mother died. It didn't matter if it was her or someone else who gave it to him. I just wanted the STD transmission to others to stop in our community, and I wanted him to know that I knew he had been unfaithful to me.

The male cousin listened to what I had to say in earnest. I told him that his cousin was in denial and to please write him a script or convince him to get tested. I had it, and he was my only partner for the last five years. I did not fault the cousin for the following statement he made. He said, "Well, Sharon, you know some STD can lie dormant for years in the body, so he very well may not have cheated on you."

I said, "No, sir, we both were tested before we began an intimate relationship. I didn't have it prior to our relationship, and neither did he."

There was complete silence. I guess he wasn't anticipating that response. Most people do not share STD medical reports prior to sexual relationships, but I do. I also added that I'd had my checkups yearly except in the last two years of our marriage because I was busy taking care of a dying mother. No sir; he cheated. He cheated within the last two years of our marriage. The exact time I needed him the most, he was being unfaithful.

The cousin made no more comments or theories. He said he would call him. I wish I could say that was the end of that, but Warden 3 kept sending me texts and e-mails regarding theories of how I got an STD. I stopped all communications with Warden number 3 again because he was no longer my problem. My good citizen duty was done, and I was able to confront that ghost of infidelity.

Genesis

Things were not always as horrible as the story above. He was actually a very sweet and loving person. Robert Earl was my third warden (husband). I had sworn off marriage. After the abuse of Warden number 2, I vowed to never give another man my whole heart again. Two years after my second divorce, I purchased a home for me and my boys. My bishop came by to bless the home and my family. As we all held hands to pray, he said something to make me drop his hand and stop him during prayer. Part of his prayer was for me a future husband. I wanted no part in another husband. They were nothing but trouble, so scared little me, did the unthinkable and stopped my bishop in midprayer. That's asking for trouble with God.

I looked bishop straight in the eyes and said, "No thanks to that husband part. Can we begin the blessing prayer again without that part?"

We had a good laugh about it, and he told me my heart would open again one day, and he was right. That was the reason I asked him to give me away at my wedding to Warden number 3. He was right; my heart opened, and I took a chance on love again.

It took about eight years, but it did happen. I met Warden number 3 at a local bar/restaurant while I was getting wasted with a couple of friends who were going through their divorce. I had no interest in a relationship. I was, at the time, dating for entertainment purposes only. If you were a good entertainer, you got a second date in rotation with the other guys I was seeing. If not, you were deleted from my thoughts as quickly as you came.

I did this rotation behavior with guys out of boredom, and it only occurred like seasons, for a few months at a time—repeat and rotate. After a season of entertainment, I would hibernate to detox myself from all the lies and nonsense behavior I participated in.

Warden number 3 approached me with the typical line: "Can I buy you a drink?" We chatted up a bit, but I wasn't interested in him because (1) I was not there to pick up a date, and (2) there was a shiny object on his left-hand ring finger. The ring was actually a fraternity ring and was upside down on his finger, which made it appear to be a wedding band.

I still was not impressed with him enough to give him my number. We exchanged information regarding our professions, to which he stated that he was retired but traveled to Cleveland, Ohio, to do contract work. At that moment, he had my full attention. Anyone who knows me knows that I am the biggest Cleveland Browns fan on this side of the Mason-Dixon Line, and I told him the same. His response was predictable and on queue. "Give me your phone number and I'll bring you some Browns paraphernalia from Cleveland on my next visit." That was it; that was the beginning of our friendship.

We casually texted over the next few months, and as promised, he had Browns paraphernalia from Cleveland for me. I met him at the local restaurant to grab a beer and receive my goodies. He wanted to come to my home and/or for me to come to his home to pick up the gifts. I was not ready for that. Besides, I did not know who this man really was. I only met him once, and I was wasted when I met him. After our meet and greet, he tried again to get me to come to his home, this time by offering to cook dinner for me. He seemed pleasant enough, and this time, I had ample time and was lucid enough to decide if I wanted to go to his home or not. He seemed harmless. Only time would tell, and it certainly did.

He was indeed a great cook. I thoroughly enjoyed our newly developed friendship. He seemed to be a good soul and could say anything and everything that made me laugh. I felt right at home. Although I felt downright comfortable with him, I wasn't anywhere near in my mind of thinking of just dating one guy. Dating one guy means you're ready to give your heart away. That was not happening anytime soon. Besides, we had developed a good friendship; no need to mess that up with a relationship. I visited him on several occasions to have one of his home-cooked meals.

However, on one visit, he asked me to pull my car around the side of his home, to which I replied, "I will not. You told me you weren't seeing anyone, and since it appears that you might be from this conversation, this will be my last visit. I don't like liars, and there is only one reason you want me to hide my car."

He quickly replied that he did not have a girlfriend anymore. They had broken up the previous month. I told him no man was worth putting my life or my fabulous mint-green mustang in harm's way. He pleaded with me not to think that way of him and that his former girlfriend Cassandra was not something to be worried about. Well, that would prove to be another lie over our five years together. She continued to be in contact with him, and he continued to entertain her calls and much more.

Cassandra called many times over our five years together. The last known call from her was on my fiftieth birthday while we were in New Orleans, our fifth year together. We were leaving the restaurant, and he asked me to get his phone out of the glove compartment. There on the screen was a missed called from Cassandra. I looked at him with such disappointment and said, "I can't even enjoy my birthday without one of your whores calling you. What could she possibly want?"

Before he could answer with the normal lie—I don't know—I said, "Oh, I know what she wants. It's almost 11:00 p.m., and it is a Thursday night. You're not supposed to be with your wife." You see, my husband, and I lived separately because of the school districts. Our cities were only about twelve miles apart though. During the beginning of our relationship, we agreed that we would comingle between the homes, even during marriage, until my youngest son finished school in my district. Also, truth be told, I had adjusted very well to living without someone all up under me all the time, and so had he. Our weekend and sometimes weekday conjugal visits would suffice for us both. We were grown folks. We could make this work. I really thought that at his age, twenty-nine years my senior, all of the foolishness would have been out of his system. But like the old saying goes, "Ain't no fool like an old fool."

For some folks, committing atrocities usually require what one of my favorite TV show's *Law & Order*'s characters would say in court regarding someone's guilt: opportunity and motive. Leaning my head against the window and staring into space as we drove back to the hotel, I thought again to myself, *This is another wasted moment of my life that I won't be able to get back.* That moment, as I've had so many times previously during our journey together, made me feel like I was at the wrong place at the wrong time and with the wrong person. Have you ever felt that way? The many happy moments we would have always turn into something like this because of his lies.

There were many episodes like that during our time together. At one point, he tried to make me feel like it was always my fault that we argued because I drank too much, as if we didn't argue when we were both sober. No, things just escalated when there was liquor—aka, my courage juice—was involved. I drank to numb the pain. I drank to drown out the lies. I drank because I was unhappy and had stayed in a relationship beyond the expiration date, and I knew it.

Drinking had never been a source of medicine for me ever—until now. Prior to Warden number 3, drinking was a ritual of celebration for me. After my first divorce, I had a drink during a sad and depressed moment, and it was the worst and weirdest feeling that I'd ever experienced before, and I never wanted to feel that way again. Pre-Google, experienced friends were your sources for knowledge. I told a friend about it, and she explained to me that alcohol was a depressant as well as a stimulant and that I should never drink when I felt depressed. I followed that advice all my life, which begs the question, why would I drink while around Warden 3 when I was depressed? I'm glad you asked.

I am a happy-by-nature kind of person. Every day is a new day, and the glass is always half full, not half empty. I did not wake up every day depressed, and I certainly did not profess the day to end badly. It just seemed to always end badly with Warden 3 causing me to become depressed. Like I said, we would always have some pretty great moments together, and I would gladly post on social media. I still remember seeing an acquaintance I hadn't seen in a while, and she asked, "Are you really as happy as your posts on Facebook indicate?"

I told her yes, which was a true statement. I—we—were absolutely happy in those moments. Now, later in the day or week, that would be a different story, depending on the warden's motives. Let me just remind folks that social media is a great tool for connecting, being encouraged, and sharing life's moments. They are called moments for a reason. You cannot compare your life or your journey on the few moments' posts you see in someone else's life. Everyone is human, and everyone has problems, some bigger than others, some more frequent than others.

When I saw his behavior and the trend of me frequently getting upset while we dated, I tried to break off the relationship, but he would proclaim to do better and blamed his behavior on trust issues, his ex-wives, and/or the fact that he's been relatively single for so long and asked that I be patient with him. I believed him. I stayed, not pardoning myself.

Once I decided to stay, I settled in like dirt, and the liquor was my life source like rain. He always blamed the alcohol for our arguments and not himself. The arguments could emerge easily because the alcohol was my courage juice to engage back and forth with him. I often thought, *I can drink with everyone else and have a good time, but not with you anymore. Why is that? Are you not my partner/husband? Are you not the one who supposed to have my back no matter what?* No, he was the enabler of the problem and an instigator of the arguments. I knew it in my soul but could not prove it until I watched the movie *A Girl on the Train*. I won't tell the plot; just watch the movie, and the following will be clear of what I experienced with my warden.

I remember an aha moment during a particular scene while watching the movie. I sat up in bed and thought, *That's what he's doing to me*, so I set up the sting. I told you I am evidence driven. I will believe everything you tell me until the evidence says otherwise. Well, the following Friday afternoon as I prepared for my weekend visit at his home, I poured light-brown-colored tea in my Macallan scotch bottle with a little scotch to mask the tea scent. I arrived at his home and immediately began the charade of drinking. We had dinner and watched a movie.

By this time, I'd had several pretend drinks. Then it started, his degrading and provoking remarks. I could not believe it, or could I? Butterfly kept her cool, though. I made subtle responses when needed. He continued. I sat in awe. He wouldn't dare speak to me that way if I were sober. He only did that because he knew that my memory would not be so good the next day after drinking. He would fill in the blanks for me. Now that I write this, was he really filling in the blanks for me or creating his version of the previous night's events. I believe the latter.

One part of me was laughing on the inside because I was finally vindicated from his lies that our arguments were on me, and the other part of me wanted to curse him out. The smarter Sharon prevailed. I kept Hurricane Butterfly at bay. After about thirty more minutes of him taunting me, I poured two more drinks from my bottle. I gave him one and said let's toast. He said, "You know I don't like scotch."

I told him it was a special blend and to do it for his Butterfly. I stared intensely as he took his first sip. The look on his face was priceless. He said, "What's this, Butterfly?"

I said, "It's tea."

"Tea," he responded. "Why you giving me tea? I thought you were giving me scotch."

I got right in his face. I replied, "I gave you what I had in my bottle. I've been drinking tea all night. I'm not drunk. I'm as lucid as one can be, and I now know how you treat me when I've been drinking. I won't have any memory problem tomorrow."

He just stared at me. He could not utter another word and hurriedly preceded to the bedroom. *This bully has just become a coward*, I thought to myself. As he walked down the hall, I proclaimed to him loudly that Butterfly just got her damn wings. That resulted in one of the two times we lawyered up for a divorce. But you know what, y'all? I still stayed married to him. I was talked into staying once again with empty promises and apologies. Again, God was showing me who this man really was, and I chose the dysfunction over common sense and not leave. I stayed, not pardoning myself yet.

I know what you are thinking. How could you get involved with someone with this behavioral dysfunction? Besides having a "type," everyone who is reading this book knows that the person you meet and the person they eventually *reveal* themselves to be later are two, three, four, five different persons. When we were just friends, he was the best kind of friend. On my final visit as a friend to his home, he tried to kiss me. You know the deacon-type kiss, the one that comes out of nowhere and try to catch you off guard. I started weaving my head left to right, avoiding him. I was like, hold up, I don't kiss my friends. If I did, I would have mono or something.

His reply was, "Well, if a hug is all I get, then a hug is what I'll take."

I'm thinking to myself, *You've been getting hugs for months. What made you think you've been upgraded to more, the chicken dinner you cooked?* To me, a kiss is more intimate than sex. It is the window to the heart's soul, so I asked him, "Why do you want a kiss from me?"

He responded that he liked me.

I said, "And so does ten other guys." Well, I exaggerated a bit.

He said, "I really like you. You know that."

I replied, "I come over here, eat, fellowship, and tell you about a date I went on the previous night, and you say nothing. I thought we were just going to be friends."

He said he wanted more.

I said, "What do you want, an exclusive relationship or to be placed in rotation with the rest?"

He announced loudly, "Exclusive, of course."

I said, "Okay, I'll be back tomorrow to go over the MOU with you."

"What? What is an MOU?" he replied?

I told him it was a legal term, an acronym for memorandum of understanding, a permission and participation contract, if you will. I told him I was tired of jumping in and out of relationships with people having unrealistic expectation, hopes, and wishes. Why bother with that when you can just tell a person what you want, what your pet peeves are, and what your deal breakers are. He agreed.

I returned the next day. We sat at his small kitchen table and sorted out our verbal MOUs to one another. My top three items were fidelity, honesty, and kinship. Although I had been married two times previously, I did not feel like kin to them. I always felt like they put me second or third, which is not the pecking order of the vows we took. I told him that although I had been scarred from previous marriages, that I was not afraid to get married again. Plus, I was not going to warm his bed until he died. Marriage would be on the table if we continued to be a good fit for one another. His top three were love, companionship (sex), and fidelity. He also stated that he went to church only once a year, Easter. In some sick way, I was delighted to hear that. My previous wardens were hypocritical Christians. We went to church faithfully every Sunday but that did not stop them from breaking our vows. I was tired of the one day a week Christian man. I didn't realize at the time that the one-day-a-year Christian men were just as bad. It felt great to actually have an adult conversation about our future relationship. I said to myself, "Self, this is going to work because y'all have agreed to terms, and there's no guessing or wishing to be had." I felt so proud of that moment. After the verbal agreement, we went to the local Hilton's bar to celebrate and dance.

After we return to his home, he engaged earnestly to get me to spend the night. I told him we just started dating today. No way I was going to spend the night. Plus, I had just finished Steve Harvey's book *Act Like a Lady, Think Like a Man*. I said there will not be any sex for at least ninety days. He looked at me as if I was speaking a foreign language. I guess I was. I told him about the book, and I also told him that we needed our STD reports. That man got up off the couch and rattled through some documents on the counter and handed me his STD reports and asked if the time that I'd been coming over as a friend counted in the ninety days. I laughed out loud and said the clock started ticking with the MOU we had earlier today. I also asked him when did he get his STD reports. He said after one of our previous conversations, in which he inquired if I was sleeping with the guys I was dating in rotation. I told him I was not because we were not serious, and no STD reports were exchanged. Until reports were exchanged, no sex would be had. He came prepared!

On one hand I was happy that he took me serious enough and got the reports, but on the other hand, I was like, this dude got a big ego thinking tonight's the night. Nonetheless, he thanked me for sharing with him about getting STD reports prior to starting a relationship. He had never been asked to do so before. He said the nurse at the VA told him that most men his age come in after the fact to get tested for STDs. He said, she told him he had a good lady friend if I required this of him. He said her name was Charlene and that he would take me to meet her one day, and he did.

We officially dated less than twenty-four hours before he broke up with me. Yes, you heard me correctly. He broke up with me! He called me the next morning and gave me excuses about his health and his age and how he was not being fair to me and put such a burden on me to take care of an older man. I knew all that was a lie. He wanted to break up with me because he did not get any cookies (sex) the night before and was not going to get any anytime soon, at least for ninety days. He was twenty-nine years my senior and was a diabetic, all information I'd had since day one of our friendship. None of this came up as an issue during our six-month friendship, during the attempted kiss, and certainly not during the oral exchanges of the MOU session we had the day before that lasted about two hours.

I laughed then, and I laugh now when I think of that phone call from that foolish man. That man who was so sweet to me as a friend and who had just become my special friend was already lying to me. He was setting the stage. Perhaps he frequently lied to me when we were just "friends." I just didn't pay any attention because I had no skin in the game, until now. At that moment, I didn't think of Maya Angelo's quote: "When someone shows you who they are, believe them the first time." I should have. I just thought it was funny and said to myself, "Oh, well, easy come, easy go."

Less than an hour had passed before he started blowing up my phone with calls, texts, and e-mails. You know I did not answer, but I did listen to the messages. His first message was how he screwed up and that he knew it as soon as he hung up the phone with me because his heart started hurting. I told myself to give him twenty-four hours in time-out before responding, and I did just that. The next day, I responded to him via e-mail, not the phone. After intentionally missing additional calls from him the following morning, I called him back and agreed to meet him for breakfast at IHOP. He was genuinely apologetic, even reading my palm as an extra player move. I fell for it. I had no clue who I was dealing with. He was sizing up my personality with that palm-reading scam.

He put on his best behavior over the next few months and treated me like a queen. I still remember the morning he gave me the name Butterfly. He called to say he had a dream about me. I thought to myself, *Here we go.* Men always try to tell you about a very sensual dream they've had about the two of you so they can get you to bed. But this was different. He said he dreamed he was at a pond that he fished in as a youth, and a butterfly sat on his lap and started talking to him. Of course, I asked, "What did the butterfly say?"

He said she told him I was the one he'd been waiting for, and his response to the butterfly was, "Is that you, Sharon?"

The butterfly responded yes. So that's how I got the name Butterfly. It was so sweet and enduring. I've never had anyone to give me a special name other than baby girl or the other per usual for black women. Other great characteristics about Warden number 3 was his mailing me beautiful Hallmark cards in the mail, even though we lived twelve miles apart and making great mixed love song CDs for me, to which we would sing in the car on our many trips on the road.

I still remember my first sleepover with him after the ninety-day mark. He brought something nice for me to wear, the usual that men do. But he also presented me with a little black box. That scared the crap out of me. I was like, *Oh, no, I ain't ready for that. I'm about to test drive only. I ain't ready to purchase yet.*

Well, the joke was on me. It wasn't a ring; it was earrings. I felt special, relieved, and pissed all at the same time. I'd never had anyone to give me jewelry before sex before. I would later find out through a girlfriend of mine that the gesture is an old OG (original gangster) player move. Too funny. With actions like that, I was falling for him but was still cautious. Then one night at a sleepover at his place, I woke in the middle of the night and asked myself, "What are you doing, Sharon? Do you love him? What are your intentions?"

I thought, *Well, I don't love him yet. He's affectionate, nice, a great friend, and frugal with money—all great attributes you want in a relationship—but still, I was afraid to love.* Then I remember what my bishop said in a sermon one time. He said you don't just fall in love with someone; fall in lust, maybe, but not love. You have to decide to love someone. That night, I looked at this man while he slept, and I declared to myself I was all in and that I would love him.

CHAPTER 2

The Shift

I can't explain this. I can only say I felt the shift. Some of you know exactly what I'm talking about. As our relationship grew, he told me that he loved me like he loved no other and that he wanted to marry me. He said he confided with his cousin that I was the one. Months later, he and that same female cousin took a trip to California to visit a dying relative. I don't know what happened while they were there, but when he returned, he was a different man and not in a good way. He wasn't perfect before he left, but he was kind and affectionate, and we were growing as a couple.

I knew he was double minded and even a liar sometimes. I remember his lying to someone on the phone, and I thought, *Hmm, that was easy for him.* I said to myself, "We're not going have any problems as long as he doesn't do that to me, and why would he? I'm his little butterfly, whom he loves and adores." Houston, we have a problem. Poor me. I was as naive as one can be.

When he arrived back in town from his trip to San Francisco, he came bearing gifts and such, but the affection and the attentiveness were off. Sure, we had welcome-home sex, but my spirit could feel the difference. I could not put my finger on it. My whole being said so. I brushed it off as jet lag or something. How could I have known he had changed his mind and heart about me. After all, he chased me for months, and we were still under the first-year mark as a couple. No big fights; nothing but great times.

As I remember this moment now, this reminds me of the biblical story of Saul and David. One season, Saul loved David; the next, David was on Saul's hit list. Unfortunately, people do change their minds about loving you for many unknown reasons. These selfish creatures do not possess the emotion of empathy and honesty. Instead, they rather keep you as a possession and see you as opportunity for their own happiness instead of creating a relationship that equally serves each person.

After a few more incidents and emotions of uncertainty, I was ready to walk away. I confronted him about the bad vibes I was receiving and his behavior. My spirit was ready for a pardon, but the rest of me was naive. He told me everything was fine and that I shouldn't worry. That he did in fact love me, and all is well. I told him that some of his actions and my spirit was telling me otherwise. I made the biggest mistake of believing him and not my spirit man or the evidence that were visible to me. Instead, I believed the hype of what everyone chants: "Don't sweat the small stuff," and "If you find a person that makes you laugh every day, they're a keeper." What about the tears or arguments that come before or after the laughter?

The conflicted Christian side of me made me stay as well—you know, the forgive the many offenses and to pray for your loved ones. I was so confused. He also knew how to appease me. If he felt I was on the edge of out of his life, he would propose a wonderful trip. The first appeasement trip was to see Beyoncé in Arizona, then St. Maarten, Hawaii, and so forth. All these trips occurred during a near-catastrophic breakup. He couldn't allow that to happen. He was the older dude with the much-younger girlfriend/wife that all of his male friends envied. Again, he saw me as opportunity, not a person.

I know all my social media friends thought he was the best ever, taking me on all these trips. They had no idea why he was being so nice to me. Don't ever envy someone's else's life. You have no clue what is going on with them the other twenty-three hours and fifty-five minutes of a day you don't see.

We had talked about Paris being our honeymoon destination on several occasions. But on this one occasion, he forgot to lie to me. As we lay in bed reading the Sunday paper, I came across an article regarding Paris. I said, "Babe, we need to decide if we want to travel to Paris in the spring or the fall for our honeymoon."

He said calmly, "I'm never getting married."

I looked at him and asked him to repeat himself. I said, "It sounded like you said you were never getting married."

He said, "I did say that, Butterfly."

I looked at him, and I calmly stated, "That's it. I knew it. You've changed your mind about me. We have been having all these little spats, and I've felt a distance from you. I could not put my finger on it before, but here it is." I packed my weekend bag so fast and headed to the door. He begged me not to leave upset. I told him I wasn't upset, and I really wasn't. I was just done with his manipulation. My spirit was very calm and peace filled my soul.

After I arrived home, I took a nice walk at the park near my home to put all the pieces of the puzzle together that had been floating in my head over the past few months. It all made sense now. I had a complete picture of our relationship—well, the relationship that he designed it to be. My cell rang. "Butterfly, are your lips still stuck out."

"No, they are not," I replied. "If anything, I'm grateful to God that He moved your lips to say what you said. I knew you had changed on me. Instead of just freeing me and allowing me to be back on the free market, you opted to keep me around like I'm your possession. I'm not your possession."

He said what all men say. "So you're giving me an ultimatum and breaking up with me, Butterfly?"

"No, I'm not," I replied. "We are not a couple anymore because you've broken the MOU we orally agreed upon. You've modified it without consulting the other said party—me—so our relationship is null and void at this moment because of your actions, not my reaction."

"Well, Butterfly, you know how I feel about getting married."

"No, I don't," I replied. "You asked to be in an exclusive relationship with me, taking me off the market from other men. I, in turn, made it clear that I would not warm your bed until you die and that if we started an exclusive relationship, then it would lead to marriage so that you could take care of me in death as well as life, and I the same. You don't get any benefits being someone's special friend.

"We've been dating each other long enough to know if we are a good fit or not, plus the fact that we've talked about where to get married, at the courthouse wearing a T-shirt and jeans, and where to honeymoon, Paris. These were real conversations that we had not just once but several times. We talked about Paris in the car, at the dinner table, and taking baths together. This I'm not getting married from you is news to me, but I'm good with that. I respect your wishes, so respect mine."

"Oh, Butterfly, please allow me to take you to Paris. I know you've always wanted to go," he replied.

See, that was his signature move, offer an appeasement trip or write me a check to get out of relationship jail with me. I didn't fall for it this time. I told him that Paris was a city for lovers, and we could not go because we were no longer lovers. I further stated that if he wanted to take me to Paris because I've never been there, then we would have to go as friends and have separate rooms.

There was a long pause. Of course, his reply was that I was being unfair to him, not allowing him to do something nice for me. Can you believe that? I'm not being nice. I advised him that he could certainly be nice to me. In fact, he could just send me to Paris by myself since he'd already traveled there twice himself; there was no need for him to come too.

"Well, Butterfly, I want to show you all the sites."

Of course you do, I thought. "That's what they have tour guides for my friend," I replied. His intentions were not to do something for me but to do something nice to me. "You want company [check], sex [check], and your twenty-four-hour-on-call nurse (check). So let's be absolutely clear: you're not offering me a trip to Paris. You're attempting to get yourself a date for Paris and all the amenities that comes with a date.

"By my calculations, I will be on the clock 24-7. That adds upward of a minimum fee of at least ten thousand dollars. The free milk is gone, Robert Earl. If you want the milk, buy the cow. Or in the alternative, cough up a larger retaining fee since this is not a true relationship."

He knew he was getting nowhere with me. Then he asked if we could still be friends and attend the state festivals that we had calendared. I said, "Yes, you're a lot of fun. I enjoy your company, and just to show good faith that I'm not mad with you, I'll certainly go with you. I understand you now and that is a good thing. And I also know where I stand with you, and I will treat you accordingly. I'm only good enough for a date but not for a wife."

After several unsuccessful attempts to get me back into a physical relationship with him and my announcement of canceling our overnight trip to Memphis to see Charlie Wilson, he had to act and act swiftly. "Butterfly, please come over to have lunch with me."

"No, thank you," I replied. Lunch did not always mean a hot-cooked meal; it meant something else hot. I reminded him those days were over.

He responded, "No, I'm serious. I've cooked some turnip greens and made my special coleslaw extra creamy like you like it, and I'll have some hot catfish by the time you arrive." He would not let me get off the phone until I agreed to come over. As promised, my food was hot and ready and absolutely delicious.

He made small talk and then excused himself to the bedroom for a few minutes. Upon his return, he had about eight printed pages he placed in front of me. I asked, "What is this Robert Earl."

He replied with a slight grin on his face, "Engagement rings. Pick one."

I said clearly, "Oh, no, I'm not doing that. You've made it very clear you don't want to be married, and I'm going to abide by your wishes. I don't want you to feel as if you were given an ultimatum." Been there, done that with Warden number 1 because of children.

"Well, Butterfly, I don't want to lose you."

"Not good enough," I replied. "You don't want to lose the sex. That is the only thing different in this season we are in."

Of course, he mustered up the saddest look with almost—and I mean almost—a tear to proclaim his love. I said, "I want to hear the words that you are not succumbing to an ultimatum, that I have not asked that of you."

His lips moved to pronounce that he loved me with all his heart and that this was not done as an act of desperation or succumbing to an ultimatum. I believed him. Poor me.

The rings were beautiful. He knew what he was doing. Every ring I picked was very expensive. I wanted to see if he was serious. "Damn, Butterfly, why do you keep picking the most expensive rings on the pages?"

I reminded him that he printed out the pages himself, not me. Then there was that same grin he had earlier. He stated that he wanted me to have something really nice because he went cheap on wife number 2's ring. She never wore it and purchased her own ring. He said she made up a lie, saying she found a ring at the airport where she worked. But he believed she purchased it herself to replace the cheap one he gave her. He said he wanted me to know he really loved me and that he was all in.

A month later, he flew to Chicago and had his jeweler buddy create the ring that looked like the one I chose. He still was manipulative. He didn't get the exact ring I wanted but close enough. It was a nice sapphire center ring with diamond trillions on the side. He was a different kind of man, so I wanted the ring to reflect it. He proposed on Christmas Eve while in bed. It was a really nice moment, but there was still a small part of me that felt he was doing this just to keep me in his life for his entertainment purposes and not for us to have a purpose-driven life as a couple. Once again, I ignored my spirit man and jump in the car with flesh.

Wedding Day

Over the next few months of planning our summer wedding, the uneasy feelings were replaced with joy and excitement. As beautiful as it was to feel this way, who knew it would be short-lived.

All I wanted was a courthouse ceremony, something simple and not complicated. After all, I've had the long white dress ceremony and reception party twice before, and so had he. This was number 3 for the both of us. However, his family wanted a traditional wedding that they could attend. Individuals were all in their feelings about our lives. I still remember his son seeing the post on Facebook about my engagement ring on Christmas Day. He gave the warden a call, not to congratulate but to express that he was upset because he was not notified that we were getting engaged that day and that he had to found out about it on Facebook.

Imagine that, a seventy-plus-year-old man having to run by his thirty-something-year-old son when he was going to propose to his lady. Not that they had that kind of father-and-son relationship, but nonetheless, he did inform the son several months prior that he was thinking of proposing soon. That's why he took the trip to Chicago. The son knew that. He just did not believe the warden would go through with it. The warden, and I had a good laugh about that.

On the son's next visit to town, he would separately try to talk us both out of getting married. Why? I'm glad you asked. His cut as an heir was about to get smaller. What other reason would he not want his father, who has never complained about his lady friend, to marry. I certainly made the warden happy, and the son never expressed any displeasure toward me, at least not when I was present. He was happy I was making his dad happy and keeping him distracted. Per the warden, the son's conversation with him was, "Dad, you told me you were never going to marry again."

To which, the warden's response was, "Well, I've changed my mind, son. It's been over a decade since the second marriage, and I love her. I don't want to be alone. I want companionship."

The son's response was that he could be his companionship. The son said he would move his wife and children from Alabama back to Mississippi so he wouldn't be lonely. The warden said, "Son, not that kind of lonely."

We laughed about that conversation. I said, "Babe, that's funny because your son had a talk with me too. He told me that you 'is' crazy and that I needed to be sure about what I was getting myself into. I assured him I could handle you." Welp. I had to watch my back on all fronts; the warden and his family.

The venue changed from the courthouse to an intimate church ceremony and reception hall after the warden announced to his friends that he was engaged. The warden's friends wanted to come celebrate with us and see who this woman was who captured his heart and got him to put a ring on it. Although the warden seemed to be excited about getting married, his focus quickly turned to the reception part of this ritual. It was going to be a grand party, he announced. Everyone was excited and coming. He could not wait to see all his friends from California, Chicago, New York, Texas, and other parts of the country. He got excited, I got excited, and before we knew it, our little one-hundred-dollar budget for the courthouse had turned into an event costing upwards of fifteen to twenty thousand dollars.

There were the normal spats about the cost, but he kept adding guests to the list. "Butterfly, did you add this person? Butterfly, did you add that person?" The list grew daily. I sold my precious little mustang to cover some cost associated with the event. If it was left up to him, he would have just put folding chairs around the walls of a cheap hall and have a bartender and a DJ and call it a day just as long as he had his party. I told him guests were spending their precious funds to come celebrate with us. No way were we going to give them nothing but the best. If we were going to have a party, we were going to have a party to remember.

I drove to his cousin's home to get dressed for our ceremony and be escorted to the chapel by her. My best friend would not arrive in time to help me dress. The cousin had a bouquet of flowers made for me. After getting dressed, we arrived at the chapel where my husband to be, bestie, a few family members, and special quests were waiting. My bishop was there too, waiting to walk me down the aisle.

As we prepared to begin the service, the cousin said aloud, "I forgot the bouquet. I've got to return home to get it." A mere ten minutes but twenty minutes round trip. I did not want to wait. It was just flowers. I said the show will go on without the flowers, but she insisted.

Here is where I write again my mistake for allowing someone to run my show. So we waited. I'm sure everyone was wondering if I was in the building. Everyone kept looking over their shoulders and at their watches. We were to begin at 10:00 a.m. but didn't get started until almost 10:30 a.m. As bishop and I waited behind the door to enter per the wedding song I chose, there through the cracked door, I see that this same cousin has taken over my wedding. She, my bestie, the warden's son, and his family are walking down the aisle before me and the bishop. I had no clue what was happening. I looked at my bishop and said, "What is going on? No one had permission to do that." The cousin had orchestrated it all without my approval. That action by the cousin was just the beginning of her inserting herself into my marriage.

Dance with Somebody

Whew, we got through the chapel service. I dismissed the action of the cousin because that was my norm, dismiss other people's action for the sake of unity and peace. Now it was time for me and my bestie to finish preparing for the reception that was scheduled for the evening. I had no wedding planner. I handled almost everything myself to save cost. More guests were checking in at the hotel. The warden kicked back and entertained the early-arrival guests at his home until it was showtime at the reception hall.

The hours passed by quickly. Before I knew it, I was behind another set of doors but this time with the warden, waiting to be introduced by our hosts as Mr. and Mrs. It had been a long day because we elected to have an intimate wedding at the chapel at 10:00 a.m. and the reception later in the evening at 7:00 p.m.

Nonetheless, I was glowing and excited even after moving non-stop to get the reception hall ready and vendors paid. I looked at the warden, expecting the same look of excitement. There was no appearance of excitement on his face. He looked drained. I asked, "What's wrong."

He said he was tired. I thought, *What a weird thing to say on your wedding day right before a big party. It's our day. You've been at your home where you could have taken a nap, but you chose to drink and entertain your friends.*

He didn't ask if I needed any help. I know in his mind, his check was his help. He should have saved his best for me. But this day wasn't about me or "us." It was about him. I knew this man. I knew him through and through.

I thought to myself, *Butterfly, he's just manipulated you again. Damn, damn, damn. The biggest manipulation of all. Got you to believe that he loves you so you'll marry him and not leave him. All that excitement you saw over the past few months was not because he was getting married to you. He was just excited for this party and to see all his friends in one place. Now that he has what he wants [marriage], a guarantee that you won't leave him, he's good.*

Well, there is something to be said about guarantees. Dictionary. com defines guarantee as:

1. a promise or assurance especially one in writing, that something is of specified quality, content, benefit, etc., or that it will perform satisfactorily for a given length of time.
2. an assurance that another's obligation will be fulfilled, or something presented as such security.

With that said, I straighten up my face that was about to be broken with tears and chanted to myself repeatedly, "Get through this night, then the next, then the next. Just do your best and see what happens." I know I'm not the only one who has experienced this. I thought, *Guarantees requires not only a promise but a fulfillment. If said party does not fulfill his end of the obligation, you can end the deal later, Butterfly. Don't let what you're feeling now steal the joy you had earlier and what you're about to have with everyone beyond this door. You have beautiful friends and family members who are waiting to celebrate with you. So what if his intentions are fraudulent. There is time to figure that out later. Go dance, girl. Dance like no one is watching.*

After our first dance as Mr. and Mrs., we worked the room. Taking pictures, giving and receiving congratulatory hugs from everyone. It was a joyous moment. I had selected several songs (Beyoncé,

Janet, and Whitney) for the DJ to play that I wanted to dance to, and dance I did. I danced with the warden. I danced with my girlfriends. I danced with high school classmates that came from far and near. I danced with my siblings too.

Mama was there. We had not received the news yet that she had cancer. It would be the following month we would find out. She was weak, but that did not stop her and that walker of hers from going all around the venue and even getting a dance in with my former employer and friend Mike. He twirled her around and made her smile. Don't ask me how a woman with a walker can be twirled around; just take my word for it. Or I can just show you the picture. Thank you, Mike!

I had the best time with my family and friends. I even managed to squeeze in a few good moments with the warden. He and his Omega fraternity brothers did a wonderful job serenading me. No tears were had all day until that happened. Tears of joy! I felt so loved. I was later told by one of the fraternity brothers who is a close friend of mine that when he approached the son to do the serenade and make it his idea, his behavior seemed off, and there was no excitement. Like father, like son. My friend thought the son would have been the one to initiate the serenade. I responded, "Yeah, he ain't happy about this union."

Now he doesn't mind me having sex with his dad, but a union— nah, he ain't happy with that. The pie of inheritance just got divided with another member. He's just here because it would look bad if he, the only child, did not attend. The root of all evil is for sure, without any uncertainty is greed. I don't remember a sincere welcome to the family by his son. It was what it was. I was a grown woman. It was hurtful, but I could handle it.

After we cut our cake, took a few more formal pictures, and enjoyed a little food, we got separated greeting some of our guest. I didn't think anything of it. I was dancing a lot, and I figured he was just hanging at the bar getting another drink or sitting at a table to rest his knees. Who knew what was happening behind my back? It would be two weeks before I would learn of what he was doing. What they were doing!

Before we knew it, several hours had passed by, and it was time to begin saying goodbyes and thank you to our guest. I had taken care of almost every detail of the ceremonies. All the warden was responsible for was securing our hotel room for the night and getting us escorted to same. He put up a fuss about the hotel's saying that it did not make sense to spend the night in a hotel when we could stay at his home. Well, his home was occupied by his son and son's wife and children. I was not spending my honeymoon night in a room next to a party of four that included children under the age of three. He grudging made the reservation but did not secure a driver to escort us after the ceremony.

We arrived at the ceremony in separate cars, and we departed in separate cars. He did not wait for me. He drove off in his car to the hotel, and I followed suit in my car ten minutes later after providing tips for the staff. All I could think of on that drive was here is one of those moments again. I'm having yet another out-of-body experience, living someone else's moment, not mine. If it were my moment, I would be snuggled in my husband's arms right now in the back seat of a limo without a care in the world, maybe ripping off some clothes. No, I'm driving myself and having thoughts of regret. The party is over.

I headed up to our room. There he is. My husband sitting on the bed taking off his shoes. He has the same look on his face as he had behind those doors. It was a stale look. Unlike the happy look he had when all his friends were around, he looked very happy while talking and drinking with them. "I'm tired Butterfly," he stated.

I told him so was I. I told him, "Let's get some rest. We've got a busy day tomorrow. My former employer Mike was giving us as our wedding gift a post Mr. and Mrs. Party at his beautiful home. All our out-of-town guests were invited so we could spend more time with them. Our honeymoon trip to Puerto Rico was several days away. We—I—delayed it to give him more times with his friends who were in town. That was me being nice and accommodating as always. Who knew this wedding was a one man's show and not a union of two? I didn't know it at the time, but it became clear to me that day and days to come.

He said, "Well Butterfly, we're married now. I guess we have to have sex. It's our honeymoon night."

I looked at that fool and said, "No, we don't if you say it like that. I'm tired like you are. Actually, I've had a long day as my own wedding planner, making sure the reception hall was perfect. I've not had a minute to myself to rest or drink like you have. I don't want to have sex if it is just something to check off your box for today."

He insisted. We had unremarkable sex on our honeymoon night, no worse than other honeymooners. If I had to guess, I would say at least fifty percent of individuals do not have sex on their wedding night. They are too tired from all the festivities. The other fifty percent of individuals are divided into two groups of those who had great sex and those who had unremarkable sex. I was fine with the unremarkable sex. Everyone has had unremarkable sex a time or two or three. I'll stop at three.

The next day was great. We had a fun-filled day visiting with his friends before and during the party at Mike's home. We fellowshipped with forty or so guests at our second party. Everything was going well until, as the evening was winding down, the warden finds me in another room and begins telling me it's time to go while I was in midconversation with a friend. Confused, I asked him, "Go where?" He said home.

I'm still confused because he's never talked to me that way, rudely and disrespectful in front of another person. He didn't ask if I was ready to go. He didn't pull me to the side to say, "How much longer should we stay, babe?" No, just, "Hey, I'm ready to go."

I had a few drinks in me so I replied, "What if I'm not ready to go?" in my Ms. Sophia voice from *The Color Purple*.

Then the lie proceeded from his lips. "Oh, Butterfly, I forgot my meds." He always used that line if he wanted to leave an event early. I told him his meds were in his pants pockets. I had placed them there. Then he looked at me with a little anger on his face and said, "I'm just ready to go. I'm tired," and proceeded to the door.

Just like that. He had become my husband and wrongfully thinking that he had a right to talk to me any kind of way now that we were married. It had not even been forty-eight hours.

All those months of behaving and being kind to me was an act. I say act because you cannot have a pattern of courteous and sweet behavior for seven or so months and then just act so rudely like that. I had just married a con man. Not wanting to cause a scene like on an episode of *The Real Housewives*, I was submissive, said my goodbyes to the host and his wife, and rode home with him. I know better than to argue with someone while they are driving. I just laid my head against the window as per usual.

I waited until we returned to his home before I let him have it. I threw my wedding rings to the other side of the room and told him I'd made a mistake in marrying him, that he'd tricked me. His deceiving ways were not gone and that he better think twice and long before ever speaking to me that way in public again. I wanted to leave, but I couldn't. My home was filled with out-of-town relatives and my adult sons. How would I explain that I needed my bed back to sleep in because I've married an idiot, and I'm getting an annulment? No, I stayed the night and slept on the floor. There would be no unremarkable or remarkable sex that night.

The Honeymoon Is Over

Puerto Rico was beautiful. We'd had enough time to make up before we arrived to the island. We could not go to Paris as previously planned because Warden number 3 had a pending indictment with the feds. He was only allowed to travel in the United States with special permission. This was going to be a new start. I hit the reset button again, all the while he's hitting his default button. He would proclaim with earnest, "Butterfly, I'm going to try harder."

All the while, I'm thinking to myself, *Why try when you can just do it, man. It ain't that hard.* Try is just an excuse word. People use the word try when they know they are not going to follow through on an action. Don't you just hate it when someone say they tried to call you. Either you did or you didn't; which is it? "Trying" in my opinion, is a mechanism for buying more time on the defective promises you've made. If I say to you, "I'll try to call you," that gives me an out.

Maybe I will; maybe I won't. But if I say, "I will call you," that means expect a call from me. The warden had no intentions of keeping his promise to me and fulfill the expectations of the husband duties that were owed to me. The marital vows say I do, not I'll try.

We had six beautiful days to enjoy in beautiful Puerto Rico. I told him for months that the only thing I wanted while in San Juan was to dine at the fancy restaurant Perla, which was located on the bottom floor of the La Concha Renaissance San Juan Resort. The pictures on their website haunted me for months. I could not wait to dine with my husband at this fabulous venue. It would create a lasting memory: the ambience, the view of the Caribbean Sea from the big windows—everything. Instead, I was left with a headache per the warden's doing. Day one: no reservations made at Perla. Day two: no reservations made at Perla. Day three: no reservations made at Perla. I woke up on our fourth day and declared that we were going. Made the reservations, and it was all set, or so I thought.

We had a great day at the beach and then headed to the room for a shower and nap before dinner. I had purchased the perfect dress for this occasion months prior. A fancy dress for a fancy place. We were near finish dressing when the warden says, "Hey, Butterfly, let's go to the bar first to have a few drinks before we go to the restaurant."

I had gotten to know this man over the last two years. There is nothing random with the words he used or his actions. He was strategizing. I said, "Robert Earl, don't try to pull any shit with me. I'm not in the mood. I've been eating all the food you brought from the local grocery store over the last few days. I ate at your favorite breakfast spot Denny's, which, by the way, cost a cool eighty dollars for breakfast! Now it is my turn. I told you about the place months ago. You should have taken me to Perla our first night here, but I let you proceed on your schedule."

"Oh, Butterfly, we're going. I just thought we enjoy a few cocktails first. I know the drinks at Perla will be sky-high," he replied.

If he really thought that and wanted to save money, he—we— would have both liquored up in the room with the spirits we had on the counter like we've done in the past. I know the routine. No, the warden was up to his signature moves. Unknown to us, there was a

Latin band playing some old-school R and B at the bar. It was great. I said to myself, "Butterfly, you're going to owe Robert Earl an apology." This is working out for the good. You're getting a little concert in before dinner. It was lovely.

It wasn't long before the warden asked the waitress for a menu. I cut my eye at him and said, "Why do you need a menu? It almost time for our reservation."

"Oh, Butterfly, I thought we'd have a few appetizers before we leave." More evidence mounting that I was not going to see the inside of Perla tonight.

I kept my cool and said okay. Shortly after we enjoyed the appetizers, the warden would proclaim to not feeling well (same scene at our postwedding party) and that he needed to lay down and take a nap. We just had a nap. "Ain't nothing wrong with you," I proclaimed. My spirit was right. I knew we were not going. I could not take myself. All my cards were maxed out because of the wedding, except my debit card. But my debit card had been compromised during our flight to Puerto Rico. Someone in Florida had my CC information and was loading up at the local Walmart. I had to cancel it with the bank.

So here I was in a conundrum—no money, no credit cards, and with a fool who was treating me like a stranger and not his wife because he knew he could. He knew I had no money! We walked back to our room, and Hurricane Butterfly appeared. I was so pissed. I even called a friend and asked him to book me on the next flight out of Puerto Rico. I promised to repay him when I returned. He tried to calm me down. I cried and begged him to make the reservation. With hesitation, he did. I told the warden I was leaving the next morning and that he could enjoy Puerto Rico by himself.

Pleading and begging commenced all night. I stayed because of the fake tears. I stayed because he would not give me the key to his home to get my car keys. I did not want to go to jail in Puerto Rico for fighting to get a set of keys. I also stayed because my card had been compromised. I had no money to get to the airport and no money should an emergency arise between Puerto Rico and Mississippi. I did not think this plan through. I would just be leaving one sinking boat to the next, owing another man something. Once again, I gave in. Not pardoning myself this time because I had not place away for myself that "mad money" wise women talk about. I never got to see the inside of the restaurant Perla. Two years later, Hurricane Maria hit Puerto Rico, and the Perla exists no more.

We returned to the states. We were back to dysfunctional normal. I was unaware at the time, but when my photographer came to see me a week later with the photos to proof, I came across a photo that so disturbed my spirit, words cannot express the betrayal I felt. Picture me in a conference room sitting across the table from my photographer as I reviewed the beautiful moments of friends and family from what was supposed to be one of the happiest days of my life. Now, picture me turning the page to a photo of him and all his family in a group photo without me. I kept staring at the picture, trying to remember when "we" took the photo and why I could not find myself in the photo.

It had become apparent quickly that they left me out intentionally. I was trying to be strong and not cry as my eyes lifted from the page to my photographer. I asked him, "Where was I."

His response was, "Sharon, I said the same thing."

We both just sat there in silence for about ten seconds as I counted every family member and stared at every couple in the picture. It seemed like forever. As I turned to the next page, I responded, "This is nothing new. The person sitting beside him thinks that she is his wife, and he treats her like it as well so he can hide assets and details that I as a wife should be privy to." I further stated to my photographer that it is my belief that his family don't believe in our marriage, and they wanted a photo of all of them together without me so when this falls apart, they won't have to cut me out of the picture. Well played, Momans; well played.

My photographer and I both laughed. As I look at the picture again today, I think to myself like I did that day, *Out of the twenty-five relatives sitting and standing there taking that photo together, no one— not even my husband—said, "Where's the bride? Where's Butterfly? She should be in this photo too." Not one. That's pretty cold.*

Everyone else had their spouse in the picture. Had I not become a spouse just hours prior? Had I not gained their last name legally? Again, nothing new. There were always moments like that occurring during our time together premarriage. He had no backbone to stand up for me. He was a user of person, not a respecter of a person. People will either see you as a person or an opportunity, not both at the same time. I could write many scenes like this that occurred, but I think you get the picture.

It has been said, "Just because you're invited to the party doesn't mean you are welcome." I was not welcome in that family. I don't miss them at all.

I waived most of my marital rights by signing the prenup he asked of me. My lawyer reviewed it and amended same to give me some protection. The warden didn't like the amendments that gave me protection and promised to provide all things without it being in the prenup. I believed him, a bad decision I will never make again. As stated in an earlier chapter, this husband of mine had already agreed to take care of me in death per our MOU. We women shouldn't have to beg a man to do what is morally right, but unfortunately, we do. Months after we were married, I told him, per the prenup, I was unprotected and that he needed to work on his will, which should have been done prior to marriage like the prenup was.

My mistake. That was a bad decision on my part. I dropped the ball. It took him six months to get a written will after I had to remind him constantly. I was not invited to the attorney's office when this document was executed, and he did not assign me as the executor. Is that abnormal? Heck, yes, it is abnormal not to have the wife as executor. I am the wife, but he never thought of me as his wife. He just gave me the title to wear and certain duties to perform but no real power. Even queens and kings in some countries still have some sort of power. This, my friend, was my biggest mistake: not fighting for my position as it was written for me per our vows. This is what I repented to God for on my resurrection day!

Once he had the will written, he called to give me a briefing on it. What I heard had me driving way past the speed limit to confront him face to face at his home. When I arrived, he was in the back bedroom on the toilet. His stomach was beginning to rumble because he knew what was coming. I greeted him at the bathroom door and said, meet me at the table and bring a copy of that bullshit of a will for me to review. I need to see for myself what you just told me on the phone.

The table is where I talked business. You cannot have a business conversation with your partner in bed; it's filled with emotions and no common sense. As I walked away from the bathroom door, I could hear him yelling, "I know what I did wrong, Butterfly, and I'll change it."

I didn't stop. I kept walking. He made it to the table with will in hand. This man, who told me I was the love of his life and that he was going to do better and make up for all the past mistakes, has assigned his female cousin—yes, the one that keeps popping up in this story—as the executor. If she could not perform her duties, then another cousin. Both cousins are around the same age as him. I'm thinking to myself, *This fool is really crazy. I'm the wife, and I'm listed as third as the executor in his will. If he died, these cousins had the authority over the estate and basically would advise me of what I can and can't have.*

I don't know why I didn't go to the courthouse the next day and file my pardon papers. Even after two years of dating and six months of marriage, this man was still manipulating me to fit his version of a relationship and marriage and not what was pronounced to us by the minister.

Vows

Wilt thou have this woman/man to be thy wedded wife/husband to live together after God's ordinance in the Holy Estate of matrimony?

Wilt thou love her/him? Comfort her/him, honor and keep her/him, in sickness and in health, and forsaking all others keep thee only unto her/him as long as you both shall live?"

Final Storm

> In the midst of her greatest heart break, she said *"all is well"*.
> The Shunammite woman's words to the prophet Elisha.
> She was the typical woman of God. Giving, kind, faithful.

These words pierced my soul as I read them and gave me a new narrative to utter from my lips. This was the title I was going to give my book, but I felt like something was missing. It was too clean. There was nothing clean about this third divorce and all actions leading up to it. And I was not as heartbroken as the Shunammite woman was speaking to Elisha. Well, I wasn't when I read this passage, but I certainly was when this storm stirred itself up. This storm, like the many we've had before, caught me off guard.

Now when I say off guard, I mean not that I wasn't aware that dysfunction could and would stir up at any given moment like scattered showers, but this was like a fierce tropical storm. The sudden arrival of it and the damage it would leave behind is what would knock me off my feet and unto my knees. Sure, there would be a forecast of it coming. And, yes, I saw it coming as always, but like most folks in storm territory, no matter what the reports say, you talk yourself into staying because you beat the last one, and it really wasn't so bad. The horrible becomes the new normal.

This storm not only was the mother of all storms we'd had, but when it made landfall, it lasted for eight days. I call this time period the eight-day lie. My husband always lied to me, which I gladly obliged because he was always, I thought, sincere with his apologies in words and deeds—key word being deeds. Yes, he paid for his sins with a check, and I gave him a receipt every time. I would even lie to myself and say, "Well, I'm getting double for my trouble just like the Word of God says, 'A lie, a lie, a lie.'" This I know was wrong, but I didn't care. And of course, it would come back to bite me. It's amazing what you will put up with and participate in when you are dysfunctional and your partner is too.

Every day when we discussed the "situation," he would tell me a new lie. And instead of just outright calling him out on it, I would cry and break down. Now this hardly ever happened. Usually, when he was caught in a lie, I was strong enough to call him out on his BS and curse him out. Not this time. There was something different this time. The pain was more intense. It wasn't the "Oh, you think you've gotten away with something again." No, I was begging him not to go forth with a business proposition. It's not a sound deal and could have legal ramifications that would not be in our best interest. He wouldn't budge. All I knew was in the five years we'd been together was that this was it unless he changed his position on the situation. After eight days of failed communication and the lie growing, I called my girlfriend, who had at one time filed for her divorce pro se, and asked if she had the template and to send to me ASAP.

I said clearly, "Don't ask me no questions, and yes, I'm sure this time." I had to say those words because we had the "divorce talk" twice before, even involved lawyers. But when it came down to filing the papers, he would talk me out of it. I told my girlfriend I was not willing to wait like I had before. I needed to file today. I was not going to let him talk me out of it. This situation was totally different and fluid. It could go sideways in any given moment. My heart finally stopped beating slow and started beating fast. My tears were replaced with anger and a sense of direction. For the first time in eight days, I could see clearly. This is the day I pardoned myself. Although I did not know it at the time that this would be the name of my book. It certainly fit.

The name for the book, *Pardon*, came to me two months after the divorce. I was attending an event, and after I hugged a dear friend, we continued to embrace by holding hands, smiling, and carrying on. Then she spoke the dreaded words I did not want to hear. "Where's Robert Earl?"

A part of me wanted to lie, like I sometimes found myself doing in the postpardon stage 1 phase when asked where he was. I would simply say, "Oh, he's fine and at home." It was the truth and a lie at the same time. He was fine; he was at his home. We were just not together.

But this time, my response was different. I was in postpardon stage 3. Before I knew it, I had guided her hand over my left hand were my weddings rings once resided and moved my head left to right, repeatedly signaling "no." She immediately knew what I meant. Her eyes swelled with tears, and then I said, "See, that's why I don't like to say such things." But truth be told, it was a small room. I didn't want to feel embarrassed should someone hear my dreadful news that I was a divorcee again!

The next morning while in the shower, I was rehearsing the day before like I often do. In doing so, that's when I came up with the name for the book, *Pardon*.

All I could remember was seeing my friend's eyes tear up and thinking, *Why wasn't I tearing up too?* Well, I had finally gotten over the outburst of tears. I was down to a once-a-month occurrence and in the privacy of my bedroom, preceded by a lot of four and six-letter words. But it suddenly occurred to me that maybe she was not only grieving my loss but the potential loss of hers or the memory of when it almost happened to her. As we all know, most marriages are on the injured reserve list. If you're not, God bless you and your great partner. But for the rest of us, welp. Marriage is hard enough for two people, but when there are extra agenda involved and outside influences such as extended family, children, job, and friends who don't know their places, it is even harder when you have a partner who will not be loyal to you and protect the sanctity of the marriage vows.

I was desperate for any narrative other than the one I had been saying when asked, "Where's Robert Earl?" I hated to say, "Oh, we've divorced," not because I hated getting a divorce. On the contrary, it was one of the most liberating days of my life. Besides feeling a little embarrassment for getting yet another divorce, I hated the looks that followed even more, that "What happened? When? Are you all right?" or the dreadful "I'm so sorry," like someone died. And I guess in some ways, there was a death.

And sure enough, if anyone would have caught me before my "resurrection," I would have looked like death hit me and hit me hard. But I was now *pardoned*. Now, again when I thought of this title, I thought of my friend and many others who I know have had some trying times in their marriages and like me stayed. It was in that very moment that I said, "Oh my god, I've just pardoned myself, but she can't. He won't let her. Or worse, she does not have the courage to do so herself." Then, like her crying for me, I cried for her and the other women I knew that came to mind.

I don't judge anyone on why they stay in an unhealthy marriage. After all, I was one of those women on three separate occasions. I pray and hope that their storms are few and less intense. I pray that their bodies be protected from some dreaded disease that their partner may encounter and most importantly. I pray for their sanity and their dear lives. The newscast reports almost weekly about women who are missing and later found dead. I use the word "partner" because some women are just as bad as men. Cheaters have no gender identity. Unfortunately, men have died of mysterious deaths at the hands of their spouse, too. I pray for them too.

There are two variations of aloneness: the kind that exist when you're alone, and then there's the other kind, the worst kind, the one that exist when you're in a relationship.

I think I also came up with the name *Pardon* because I was studying the Old Testament with haste and conviction. I was hurting so bad, and I knew of one other character in the Bible besides Jesus who had been hurt, lied to and about, and betrayed like me; it was Joseph. I wanted to refresh myself with his story knowing that his ending turned out okay.

You see, when you're in the middle of a devastating life moment, you really don't know if you'll be okay. You say it to yourself. Others say it to you also, but deep down inside, you wonder, will you? Will you bounce back from yet another life event? Yes, yes, you will. And as you may or may not know, Joseph's story turns out pretty well also. He is pardoned by the Pharaoh and ends up getting a pretty cool job that not only causes him to have fame, influence, and wealth but enough wealth to take care of his immediate and extended families. He becomes the prince of Egypt. Imagine what or who you will become once you are pardoned! I hope reading my story will help you heal and remind you that you will get through this season.

CHAPTER 3

Former Wardens

I've not only once but three times pardon myself. Before I get to my journey with Warden number 1 and number 2, allow me to define warden. Merriam-Webster describes a *warden* as an official charged with special supervisory duties or with the enforcement of specified laws or regulations. Hmm, I don't know if you laughed when you read the definition or gasped for air for the sheer irony of it all but I did. Let's break this down. From a biblical standpoint, this is all to be true. God officially ordained the man to have charge over us, but this thought was to be in our best interest. But we know what man has and what man does with *power*; he takes full advantage of it.

Now the later of the definition is what, I guess, causes me to laugh. I'm just reminded of how at specific times in my relationship/ marriage, the specified laws and regulations were amended and/or removed from the books without any sufficient notice to other said party. That said party would be me!

Warden Number 1

Wife. I became a wife at the age of twenty-two but a mom at the age of nineteen. We met when I was sixteen and he was eighteen. I, a junior in high school, snagged a college dude. That certainly boosted my confidence. I met him at a Campus Crusade for Christ gathering.

49

He was the cool, good looking guy with the Jheri curl. Y'all look that up if you're not old enough to remember what hairstyle that was. He was my first love. I'm trying to remember when we fell in love. It is just all fuzzy now while writing this book.

When he asked me to be his girl, he did confess that he already had a girlfriend back home in Arkansas. Of course, I told him no way I was going to be involved in breaking up a couple. He lied, like most men do, and said that the relationship was basically over already and that he didn't want a long-distance relationship. That was the very first lie that I know of that he told me. I advised him to get his affairs in order and then give me a call. Yes, that's how I talked at sixteen years of age.

On his next trip home, according to him, they talked and agreed to break up, and she cried, and he felt really bad about it, but that he was glad it was over. Well, truth be told, it was not over. He would continue to see her over the years. Yes, while we were dating, while we were married, and while he was married to his second wife, which, by the way, all occurred while she was married to her husband.

Thin Line between Love and Hate

The news of his cheating on me with the former girlfriend, who eventually became his wife number 3, came from his mom. She spilled those beans. She knew we were having some issues like all young couples with two small children and were going through an estrange period in our relationship. Like most of us, your heart believes that things will work out. After all, we had two beautiful sons under the age of four. But it wasn't going as planned.

Although she loved me and her grandsons, her call was a bit self-serving. The call was a total shock. "Sharon, please work it out with brother. I don't want him to be killed." That was an odd statement, I thought. As she continued to speak, it became clearer. "Please work it out with him," she continued. "He spent the night over there with Cynthia in her trailer. She's separated from her husband, but they are still legally married, and I don't want brother to be killed."

That was his nickname, brother. I had to take a seat. You mean to tell me this no-good lying son of a biscuit eater is laid up with this trailer tramp.

He had injured his back at work. And since he was on leave from work for a few weeks, he told me he wanted to go and spend some time with his mom. Who would have thought it was a rendez-vous with a trailer tramp? Obviously, his back injury was not that bad. And obviously, this was planned. It was all a lie to get out of town to see her and spend time with her.

Again, the signs are always there when something is not right. I still remember times when he would tell me he had to send his mom some money. I would say, "She sure does need a lot of money lately."

To which he would snap back at me and say, "That's my mom, and I'll send her whatever she needs." It was never, "Babe or wifey, my mom needs help. Let's look at our budget to see what we can do." No, it was all secretive. That's because he was hiding the affair. I could have called his mom during those times to confirm that he was sending her the money, but I know how mothers love their sons and will lie for them. I have a little policy. Never ever invite or volunteer people to lie to you. If they do it on their own accord, well, that's on them, but if you ask questions and receive a lie, well, that's on you when you already know the answer to the question.

It was very clear at this moment that when he was sending money to Arkansas, it was not always his mom; it was to her. I suspect his mom had a mother-son talk, and he reluctantly came back home to be with his family as if the affair in Arkansas never happened. His mom's plea to me, along with wanting my boys to have a father, kept me in the relationship at that point in my life, and it would be a few more years before I would be able to *pardon* myself. A few years don't seem like long, but when there is discord, dysfunction, and disloyalty, a few years can feel like a decade.

Truth be told, I had rights to pardon myself from him earlier in our relationship because of infidelity, twice that I am aware of before the third affair with the trailer tramp. Let's start at the beginning. As a young Christian couple, we pledged to wait for marriage before sex. Well, guess who did not keep their end of the pledge. Yep, the warden. I think he only confessed to me that he slept with the female roommate in the off campus college apartment was because she was going to spill the beans soon. What other reason would he have to confess? Good heart? No. Remorseful? No. Men only confess when they are caught or about to be outed.

I noticed weeks before his confession of his dirty deed to me that the tension in air at the apartment was thick. I didn't know why, and of course, me being green as I was, I did not put two and two together. The female roommate, who at one time had been so nice to me, had become public enemy number 1. She would roll her eyes and sometimes snarl while I was there. I chalked it up to PMS or just a bad day in class. I had no idea she had slept with the warden and wanted him all to herself. So I'm assuming in her mind, break up with her and be my man, or I'm tell her about us. But he would beat her to it and confess with all the fanfare of tears and snot.

I think I blocked it out at first because I had no reaction. Then he said it again because I had no response. I still didn't believe it when I heard it the second time because we had an oath—a pledge—not only to ourselves but to God. I just could not believe it. So here comes the pretty lie from him to make it right and her fault. He said that almost every day when he would come home from work or school, that she would flirt with him and basically throw herself on him. Okay, what the hell does that mean?

My poor little self. I was only eighteen. I had no clue whom I was dealing with, a freaking liar! I can't remember everything I said to him at that time—perhaps, how did your clothes come off? Did she beat you up and take your clothes off? I know they don't make blue jeans with a separate slipper for a penis to fall out. How did you get inside of her? I don't know if I were brave enough to say all that back then, but I sure as hell would say it now. At that moment, I remember the pain—still to this day—of the first hairline crack in the foundation of my heart.

Pressure on All Fronts

After that episode, I, like most girls at that age, felt the pressure to have sex. Although we made a pact not to have sex until marriage, it was clear that he was not going to keep his pledge. And since we loved each other and were going to get married anyways, why not begin the bedroom part now. Who would find out? He had an off campus apartment, and I was not going to let that hussy out do me and sleep with my boyfriend when I perfectly could. I made sure that the days I visited the apartment that I would wear something really tight to show off my curves or my flat stomach. None of that church-girl Campus Crusade for Christ clothing. I wanted her to know that her services were no longer needed.

I still remember her returning to the apartment while we were there. I appeared from the bedroom feeling empowered and asked her if she had anything cold to drink because I was mighty thirsty. I even said to her, "I hear you know how good he is." I wanted her to know that I knew their secret so she could stop with the looks and the snarls and thinking she had something on him or over me. I laugh at myself now. Truth be told. I was mad as hell. But I could not let it show. The evolution of Hurricane Butterfly would be years away.

I could have kept every bit of my dignity and virginity and slapped his face and ended the relationship when he broke our pledge to one another. But I didn't. *I had invested two years into this relationship*, I thought. That's one of the lies we say to ourselves. I've invested XYZ amount of time with this person, so we will stay together.

So what? What was the return? A broken spirit. We women are not good with relationship math. Two years plus lies plus cheating does not equal happy life. So think very carefully when you tell yourself to stay because of what you have invested. Your return is not good at all, my dear. As they say in the stock market, sell!

Who would find out our secret that we were having sex? I thought. God don't play! Well, within a year, everyone would because I became pregnant with our first son—nineteen and pregnant. I remind my son all the time, he belongs to me, assigned from God. He just came earlier than originally planned. Becoming a mother was my greatest calling. I loved my son. Pretty soon, I was convinced that we should have another child so our son would have someone to grow up with. I did not agree about the timing of the request because we were flat broke and college dropouts, but I agreed. After all, we were partners who loved each other and would be together forever. So I thought.

Guess Who's Coming for Dinner

The first affair caught me off guard; the second one did not. Everyone has a radar that goes off in your head that something is not right in your relationship, but you ignore it because there is no evidence to back up your emotions. I am an evidence-base-driven person. I don't believe in theories or random. Back in the day, men did not have Facebook, Snapchat, Tinder, or smartphones to help them cheat. All they had to work with was a pager and a quarter to call the side chick on the corner pay phone booth.

I remember when the uneasy feelings started reoccurring. He would suddenly have to go to the store more often than usual on the weekend. That was our time together since he worked the night shift and I the day shift. We did everything together until now. Now with such haste, he had to randomly go to the store because we needed something or he forgot to pick up something. I would say, "Hang on. Let me comb my hair so I can go too."

He would say, "Oh, I'll be right back," which sometimes was not true. Sometimes, it would be a few hours before he would return. Since we didn't have cell phones, there was no way of him contacting me, saying he was running late or had to run an extra errand, only a pager, to which he would not return my call.

The times he returned home later than expected; he made up the excuse that he was visiting the couple we were close too. Well, that did not make sense because they were our son's godparents. They always wanted "us" to visit to see their godson. I knew something was going on. I could not confirm anything, but nothing is random and not like that for almost a month. I remember one day saying, "I'll get him today." I sat on the couch, pregnant with our second child, dressed in my bathrobe and a hat on my head. He walked toward the door without warning as before, saying, "I'll run to the store."

I said, "Give me a second and I'll go with you."

He said the normal, "I don't have time to wait for you to get dressed. I'll be right back."

I whipped off that hat and robe and said, "Oh, I'm ready."

He was not expecting that. His eyes bucked. Turns out, he was not going to the store. He was going to his side chick's house, a mutual friend of ours. Imagine that, ladies. And since the only means of communication was through the phone, he could not cancel his rendezvous.

He stopped by a store for pretense then stated that he needed to go by the mutual friend's home to drop off some information for her. She was trying to get a job where he worked. When we arrived, he said, "I'll be right back."

To which I said, "Oh, no, I haven't seen Penny [that's not her name; I don't remember] in a while. I'm going to say hi." I could see the sweat on his forehead.

As we walked down the hall to her apartment door, he tried to walk faster than me. I kept up. One son in my belly and another, my one-and-a-half-year-old, on my hip. As we both arrived at the door together, she opened the door with a big smile happy to see him until she opened the door all the way, and she saw me. They both looked foolish. She had dinner ready and everything.

Yes, I ate. I sure did. We stayed about an hour. I kept my eyes on her every second. I handed him our child, and I followed her every move around her apartment. Amazing how I kept my temper under control back in those days. Hurricane Butterfly had not evolved yet. I still remember her saying to me, "The pregnancy is making your nose wide," which was a lie.

I kept my cool and asked for seconds. All I've ever gotten throughout my pregnancies were compliments. You had to look hard at me to see if I was pregnant. I held my weight well, and there was no swelling anywhere. A woman will try to tear you down if you stand in the way of something she wants, even if it is your man. He was stuck with me because we had one son and one on the way, and there was nothing she could do about it.

Truth be told, there was nothing I could do about it. I could not yet pardon myself. That was a long ride back to our apartment on the other side of town. That hairline crack in my heart would take another hit. Although it was not truly confirmed that night that he was having another affair and with her, it would be confirmed soon enough.

Not Me

I arrived at the doctor's office for my monthly prenatal checkup. Dr. Sullivan and his nurse entered the room, completed the exam, and explained to me that the results from my last visit. He said, "You're doing fine. Your weight is under control, and you have chlamydia."

I had never heard that word before. Sex education and Google were not readily available back in 1988 for me, and of course, there is that part about me being green. I had no clue what chlamydia was. So me being me, I said, "Is that similar to my anemia?"

I'll never forget as long as I live the way the doctor and nurse both looked at each other, then back at me. He didn't answer my question immediately. He asked me to get dressed and meet him in his office. I thought that reaction was weird, but I did not understand how weird it would get in the next five minutes in his office. I sat in his guest chair, and he began to speak as he picked up his prescription pad and began to write, "Chlamydia is a sexually transmitted disease."

To which I said, "Well how do you get it?"

He said, "Through sexual intercourse."

I said, "Well, I've only been with one person."

There was that look again on his face that he had given me in the examination room. It took a minute, but when it kicked in, I felt numb from the top of my head to the bottom of my feet. He realized I finally understood. He asked, "What is your partner's name?" I replied. He tore off both prescriptions and gave me further instructions.

As I sat there, numb and furious, I kept telling myself to move. Get up out of this man's office. He has other patients to see. But I could not move. I finally jerked my body to move and walk the walk of shame through the hallways and then to my car. I knew that only Dr. Sullivan and his nurse knew of my big health news, but I might as well been wearing a T-shirt stating that I had chlamydia.

How could this happen? I was the good girl. I waited until I was eighteen to have sex. I only had one partner. How in the hell does this happen? After my nice cry in the parking lot. I contemplated my options. I had none. Mother of one and one on the way, one car between the two of us, and me working a part-time job—what was I to do? Go back home to Mom? No way. She had raised five of her eight children and was raising some grandchildren like her mother raised her first three children. I was not about to be another burden on her.

She had warned me about him. What did she know, I thought as a young adult. As I would learn later in life, it's not what an older wiser person knows; it is what they've experience in life that they try to help you make better decision than they did. These are my experiences. I boldly and transparently share them with you so you can make better choices than I did, or in the interim, improve on your choices.

I arrived at our apartment just in time for him to wake up and get ready for work. He worked the night shift. Oh, yes, the best shift there is for a cheater. There was no set schedule at work for the shift to end. The shift could end at 3:00 a.m., 4:00 a.m., or even 7:00 a.m. I did not keep tabs on him like that. I sat on the couch and asked him to join me. I said, "I have something for you." I had not made up in my mind how to ask how in the hell this happened or even to fight. I was scared and broke—scared of the truth, scared to go into premature labor, just scared.

I handed him the prescription with his name on it and asked him, "How did this happen?"

He replied, "You must have cheated on me," and walked away.

That was all I got. Really, man, that's all you got.

As mad as I was, I had time to calm down driving home, plus I was pregnant. If he really thought it was me, he would have yelled like I wanted to. He would have asked a million questions like I wanted to. He would have said, "Is the baby mine?" No, his cowardice did the talking for him when he took the prescription and walked to the bedroom to get dressed for work like nothing happened, nothing but guilt written all over it. My mind and heart had to deal with the confirmation that he had cheated again and with our friend, Penny.

Plan B

No pardon for me yet. I had to stay, and stay I did, but I made up in my mind; it was time to get a plan. He kept pressuring me to get a washing and dryer. I refused. I did not want to make a new bill commitment. I did not know when I was going to leave; I just knew that I would one day, eventually. I was going to serve the remainder of my sentence with this warden and leave soon.

So as I continued to serve my sentence, we welcomed our second son. From the time of my learning of this second episode of infidelity and the birth of our son, our relationship had become estranged, to say the least. We were still together playing the couple's role with the birth of our new son until one day, he walked in and started clearing his clothes out of the closet. I was awakened from a nap with our four-week-old newborn and assumed he was getting his uniform for work when I noticed he had a lot of clothes in his hand. With blurred eyes, I asked, "What are you doing?"

His simple reply was, "I'm leaving you."

He didn't say, "I'm leaving y'all" (me, our eighteen-month-old son, our four-week-old son). No, he said, "I'm leaving you." It was personal and pure evil. I had no job and had not even gone back for my six-week checkup. What kind of man does that? A foolish one.

What was I supposed to do now? But God! At that time, my military brother had returned to Mississippi and was temporarily staying with us. When the warden left, my brother offered to stay longer than he planned to help with the bills and such. I told him that God would make a way, and make a way He did.

As painful as it is to be lied to, cheated on, and disrespected, God has you. I had two options after that happened: stay in that apartment and have a woe-is-me pity party and be mad at the world for this unfair thing that has just happened to me or square my shoulders up, put on some lipstick, and go find a job. A job indeed is what I found. It was a part-time job at the local Pizza Hut, but it was more than that. It was who God had placed there for me to meet that would be on my journey for the next few years of my life.

I was a college dropout, barely twenty-one years old, with a work history of only fast-food restaurants. That income only affords you the fear you have of living paycheck to paycheck, the codependence of other people such as the "wardens," and the state's welfare system. Both are the same in my opinion. It was good that the warden left me. It thrust me out of his nest. I was going to leave at one point anyway, but this propelled me.

Upon working at Pizza Hut, I met the loveliest young lady Angela. I cannot remember her last name. I hope she finds a copy of this book and contacts me. I would love to give you another hug my sister. This girl was my rock. She welcomed me to Pizza Hut, trained me, and mentored me. I'll never forget it. I was so wounded and fragile at the time, and she was there for me. She was, like I am now, a straight-up hustler—work, work, work, work, work. She worked at Pizza Hut part-time, worked at Trustmark Bank full-time, and attended night school at Draughon's Business College downtown. She encouraged me to enroll, and I did. It was a business school, a school to train secretaries and executive assistants. I loved it, and I loved hanging out with her.

After completing my courses at Draughon's, and through her connections at the bank, I landed a job. I was elated. My first corporate job at Trustmark National Bank. My first corporate job was a bank teller. I was about to make the best money in my life and have benefits. Heck, I just giggled inside at orientation. Everyone remembers their first real job, the one where you received a salary, paid time off, vacation days, and benefits. It was wonderful. Not only did I follow Angela to Trustmark, we both landed jobs at Steak and Ale Restaurant. It was a five-star restaurant back in the day. I'm really showing my age now.

She of course, being as fierce as she was, was employed as a waitress. I, on the other hand, still timid, was a hostess until that fateful night when an employee did not show up for work. I was thrust into the position of server. I was so scared and intimidated. The pros made it look easy. There was so much you had to remember. After four hours of becoming the newest server at Steak and Ale and earning in one night what I made in two weeks, I suddenly became a pro as well. I was ready for the world of serving. All of this takes place over a period of two years. What I write next will shock you; it shocks me thinking of it.

After warden number 1 left me, our eighteen-month-old son, and our four-week-old son, he returned two weeks later. I don't know what or who made him return. I had been on my own just enough time to get my bearings together and my feet on the ground. Two weeks is a long time to a woman scorned. God had me, and I knew it. I just needed to keep getting up every day, expecting great things to happen and making sure I was a participant in making it happen. I was scared no more.

You want to cheat, cheat. You want to leave, leave. It does not matter. I had not landed the job at the bank just yet. I allowed him to come back because my little part-time job at Pizza Hut was not going to be enough to stay in our apartment, and I would have had to get on welfare for food and insurance and go stay with a relative or my mom. I picked my poison, him. It wasn't pretty. It wasn't ideal. But it was my present situation. I made the best of it. He was my babysitter while I attended school at night because he worked the late shift. It was an awesome feeling.

When school was cancelled, I still got dressed and pretended to go. I met up with Angela or some other friends to have a drink. It felt good to be an adult and hang with adult friends. Previously, he was all I had. It felt good to have my own identity and do something by myself with my friends as he did. Truth be told, it felt good to lie to him. I know I'm not supposed to say that, but it was the truth. I had a smile on my face walking out that door. I said, "Hmm, this must be how he feels when he leaves me home alone with the kids to go play." I know it was not right. It was my temporary truth.

Having a great job and a side hustle job gave me enough financing and courage to pardon myself. My pardon would not last long, though. While we were separated, he, of course, missed the "family unit" we had, and I would be lying if I did not say he was put under pressure from family and friends for us to get back together. And so was I. I fought it as much as I could, but when my youngest began to walk, the thought of him missing that moment hurt my soul, and I wanted my children to know their father. I returned to the warden's care. I thought it would be best for all. I was mistaken. Two unhappy parents do not make a happy childhood experience.

I stayed. I stayed with Warden number 1 from age sixteen to twenty-six. We even got married when our youngest son turned two. I know what you are thinking. I'm thinking it too while I write this. But at age twenty-two, I just wanted to do right by my boys and do what most women do—stay for the sake of the children.

Four long years, I put up with mostly the same behavior. I don't remember every misbehavior, but one particular scene comes to mind that still makes me laugh. Back in the 1990s, there was a hip-hop group called the 2 Live Crew. The band had made their appearance in our city. The warden knew I did not care for such foolishness of that particular band. Instead of just asking or even announcing he wanted to go to the concert, he decides to pick a fight. That's what men do when they want to get out of the house without permission.

I know the following will seem all too familiar to some. He picked a fight with me about something very irrelevant and then stormed out of the house. I thought to myself, *That was odd*, not realizing what just happened or who was in town. It wasn't until I saw on the evening news that I realized where he was. Hours later after he arrive home, I asked, "Did you have a good time at the concert?"

He wasn't expecting that; he was expecting a fight. *Why fight again?* I thought. So you can have another excuse to run off. I just played the hand I had for those four years. It's all a blur.

At age twenty-six, I had enough of his promises to leave the night shift and work days so I could return to college. He knew my dreams of becoming an attorney. He was not supportive, and I got behind on my dream. There were still occurrences of his coming home hours after he had left work. After I saved enough "mad" money to be on my own, I met with a divorce attorney and without a clue, presented the paperwork to him. I advised him that he could get a lawyer or that we could use same attorney and save money. We did just that. But before the ink was dry, he finally changed his schedule to day shift, started cooking more meals and helping around the home, and purchased me lingerie and perfume without its being a special occasion. Imagine that. I didn't fall for it. Ten years together—from age sixteen to twenty-six—and three affairs later, I was long overdue for my pardon, and pardon I did.

Unfaithfulness

He was tall and very handsome, the football-player type. I admired his good looks from afar. After all, he was a married man. He and his wife would frequently visit the restaurant I worked. I had no clue he thought of me any way other than his server. His conversations with me were always casual, even when he visited the restaurant by himself. He got a promotion and moved to another state. Almost a year had passed since I'd seen him. During that year's time, warden number 1 and I divorced.

One night, during a shift at the restaurant, one of his friends dined in my section. He noticed that I was not wearing my wedding rings. He asked, "Did you leave your jewelry at home?"

I replied, "I don't wear a lot of jewelry to work."

He responded, "No, I mean your wedding rings."

I laughed and said, "That ship has sailed. I'm divorced."

He just smiled slightly and said the following: "Oh, I know someone who will be glad to hear that."

I was confused. I said, "Who?" I will change the name of this person and call him Randall. So back to the conversation.

He said his name and stated with emphasis that Randall had a huge crush on me. He also told me that Randall asked him to come to my job to check on me, and that's why he's been coming over the last year.

I was shocked to say the least. I responded and said, "Man, Randall is a married man. I just divorced a cheating man. I'm not getting caught up in something like that. It's hurtful and disrespectful."

He said, "No, Randall is divorced too. Timing is great, isn't it?"

I thought, *Yeah, he's cute and all, but I think I would feel weird about the whole thing.*

He kept talking, telling me how long Randall had a crush on me and that I would break his heart if I did not give him an opportunity to at least call me. He also added that he would have to keep coming back to the restaurant and sit in my section and order one beer and take up my table if I did not give him my phone number. I gave in. I remember him leaving and telling me how happy I was going to make his friend.

"Hi, Sharon, this is Randall," the voice said on the other end of the phone. Y'all, this was a landline. Cell phones were not available to the masses at this time.

I said, "Hey, you, it's weird to hear your voice." I was so nervous. I rehearsed in my head all the things his friend said. I was thrilled to have someone feel that way about me again, especially being in that postdivorce mood, feelings of being unloved, unworthy, and devastated. But here was a man who was crushing on me. My toes tingled at the thought.

As I calmed myself down, I began to listen to his words that sounded like poetry to me. He told me he and his wife divorced because she did not want to move to the new state he was in. He said he was devastated. I, being in a devastated mind also, sympathized and thought to myself, *How cruel of her.*

After we talked a little longer, he said what I wanted to hear. When can I see you? I told him whenever he was in town. He advised me that he frequently came back to Mississippi to see his children at least twice a month when his job allowed him. I proceeded to give him my address. To which he said, "I already have your address."

63

I paused and said to myself, *What the hell.*

He said, "I had my buddy run your plates."

OMG, nothing uncommon for law enforcement men. That's what they do, so I left it alone.

He made reservations at a very nice restaurant. I was so nervous when he arrived in my driveway. I had not seen him in a year. Here he was, this man I secretly had a small crush on and him me. I met him at the door and could not believe it. We hugged for what seemed liked ten minutes. He said, "It's so good to see your again."

I said, "Likewise."

I talk really fast when I'm nervous and say weird stuff, so I had a conversation with myself prior to his arrival. "Be quite, Sharon, and let him do the talking." I wore my best fitted dress. After all, he'd only seen me in the restaurant's employee shirt and my work jeans. I wanted to look fabulous for our first date. I think I nailed it. He couldn't stop staring.

We had a fantastic night and agreed to start dating. We talked about me coming to his new state he lived in, his flying me in or driving. Either way, he would pay. Our plans were to sightsee, shop, visit his church, and meet his pastor. I was like, *Wow, he really does like me. Who introduces someone to their pastor?*

I had the best time when I visited him, but for reasons to be revealed later, I never got to meet the pastor. There was always an excuse. I thought maybe he was feeling guilty like I was for being a fornicator. See, we both were good Christian folks. We were not supposed to be engaging in premarital sex. He read his Bible to me and talked about our faith, but like most men, they want their cake and eat it too. No matter his beliefs, sex was on the table.

We were having the best eight-month relationship. Then Christmas rolled around. He told me he was going to see his family in Illinois. I was disappointed that we were not going to spend our first Christmas together but understood that he rarely got to see his parents and extended family.

Again, this is the time of no cell phones to the general public. We had the next best thing, pagers. For you young, young readers, that was a wireless telecommunication device that received and displayed alphanumeric and/or voice messages. In those days, you had to actually wait for someone to communicate with you if you did not have landline number to where they were staying. And I did not have an Illinois landline to reach him. He explained to me before he left that he would be at multiple relatives' homes and that he would page and call me accordingly. Made sense to me. After all, we were in love!

However, there were two days that no communication was had between us, one being Christmas Day. I was furious and hurt, but he explained it all to me once he called. He told me that he had a friend who was addicted to crack and that he had to do an intervention with him that required him be locked in a hotel room with his friend so he could not leave and buy drugs. He said his friend's life was at risk. I felt so bad. I started crying and thought what a wonderful man to sacrifice his time for a friend like this. I thought to myself, *Surely, he is the one.*

The very next month, I had to go purchase my favorite pair of Hanes pantyhose at the mall. While heading to the hosiery section of the department store, there she was, the ex-wife. I thought to myself, *Did he tell her he was dating me? How did she feel about that? How did I feel running into her? Well, Sharon, you're going to be stepmom to his kids one day, so you might as well get this over with.*

All these thoughts were going through my head, then I chickened out and thought, *Not today. I don't want to deal with this today. Suppose she was not happy with us being a couple, and she would make a scene.*

As I turned away to go in another direction, I heard her voice. "Hey, Sharon, how are you doing, girl?"

I was three, four, five clothes racks away from her. How did she see me? It was fate. As I slowly walked toward her, she was surprisingly smiling and reaching to give me a hug. I thought, *Oh she's taking this really well if he told her, or she's in the dark of our new relationship.* So I played it cool.

"What have you been doing with yourself girl?" she said.

I replied, "Enjoying the holiday, you know, the normal. What about you?"

She smiled with joy and told how she and Randall had a good time in Illinois for the holidays, that his family had not seen their little girl since she was born. My heart started beating really fast, but I calmed myself down to get more information. I smiled back at her and asked her how dear old Randall was. I had a million thoughts in my head, and they all involved cursing him out. It was clear that she knew nothing of our relationship. Why should she? They were still married. I didn't know he was married, and she didn't know he started a new relationship with me. I'm sure he thought there was no chance that we would run into each other because I had quit the job at the restaurant and began working as an administrative assistant at a medical office—until tonight.

She continued with more intel. After he moved to the new state, they decided to wait a few years for her to come up since they had no family there, and he would be working most of the time. As you can see, a completely different version of what he told me several months prior. I stood there patiently getting all the intel I could get. After I purchased my pantyhose, I drove that Ford Probe as fast as I could to get to my landline. I dialed his pager and put 911 in the text. I could not wait for him to finish his shift. His job required him to be undercover a lot. I didn't care. I needed to talk with him ASAP. "Hello, babe, I got your text, what's wrong."

I replied with anger, "Guess who I ran into at the mall."

There was silence. The charade was over. In a very low and sad voice he replied, "Melissa."

I've changed her name as well. I screamed at him and asked him, "How could you do that to me? How could you put my life in danger and my children?"

When he came to visit here in Mississippi, he stayed with me. When I went to his state, I slept in their bed, sat on their couch, cooked food on their stove, showered in their bathroom. I was so angry. Suppose she found out and "snapped" on us and killed us in bed while we slept in a jealous rage. My children would be without a mom.

I continued to scream at him while tears flowed immensely. Suppose she kidnapped one of my boys in revenge. All sorts of thoughts rang through my head. He had no logical excuse, just the typical ones that men use. "You were never in any danger. I would not let that happen to you."

I'm thinking, *Dude, you are not with me one hundred percent of the time. What are you talking about? We live and two different states. Do you have some kind of presidential detail with guards on me 24-7? At best, you can protect me only four days out of a month on your visits to me and vice versa.*

I was furious. I reinstated how she could have killed us in our sleep. I said, "Suppose she just missed you one weekend and decided to surprise you and walk in on us. You never saw a possibility of that ever happening?"

He replied, "No, she would never drive up here because she never has."

Like there is not a first time for everything. I told him I never wanted to see him again and that he made me a mistress by default. He never asked me if I wanted to be a mistress. I didn't, but there I was, all in the thick of it. I could never wash that moment away from my life. He thought that by seeing me in person would make it all right. He said he would be in Jackson in four hours. I told him not to bother, but he came anyway.

I went to the clubs to hang with friends so I would not feel sorry for myself. When I returned home, he was there on my doorsteps at 2:00 a.m. We talked till the sun came up, and I sent him on his way. I told him he had some nerve cheating on his wife, especially knowing what I just experienced with my ex-husband. He knew I would never sign up for that. So he did what men do and lied to me so that we could have a relationship. He had no plans to divorce his wife. Perhaps he thought after I fell madly in love with him, I would go with the flow of being his mistress. I told him I could not ever trust him again, and I certainly was not going to be anyone's mistress.

After that day, he continued to leave messages on my answering machine with the song "Breathe Again" by Toni Braxton playing in the background. But I never spoke to him again. That Sharon knew how to pardon and pardon quickly.

Never Say Never

He was my dancing partner at the local club. His pseudonym name will be Jake in this story. I started hitting the clubs after my first divorce. Looking back, that was completely the wrong course of action. I think it is a rite of passage for most first-time divorcees, male or female. It's the place you go and pretend to be someone else, and no one is the wiser. I had never gone to clubs ever in my life until I got a divorce. I began working some weekend shifts at a restaurant to make extra cash during that time. All the servers brought a change of clothes to hit the clubs after the shift. No need for me to go home to an empty house when the boys were with their dad for his weekend. As it turns out, warden number one was not that heartbroken over our divorce during this time. He began a relationship as well and moved in with his soon-to-be wife number two and her children. Everyone was getting on with their lives. I was devastated and lonely.

Sometimes I hung out with the crew at whatever spot was open at twelve, one, or two in the morning, or I would sometimes hit my new spot called the Pinnacle. It was a small club with the usual local suspects. I wasn't going to pick up Mr. Feel Good or anything like that—farthest thing from my mind. I just didn't want to go home to an empty house and feel sorry for myself. Per the divorce decree, warden 1 had the boys every other weekend. That became Mama's time for herself.

I knew the clubs were not the place for me. What could come of it? But I went anyway and faithfully. I knew within, it would only be for a season. If someone asked what I did on the weekend without the boys, I proclaimed with a smile that I went to the club. I felt liberated. I had been a good girl all my twenty-something life and was done wrong by men. I wanted to see what the other half was doing in these streets. My girlfriends or cousin's response to me would be I would have gone with you if you called. I would reply, "No. If I'm going to hell, I'm not taking you with me."

My clubbing did not keep me from going to church, though. Yes, this little Christian gal still went to church on the weekends I had my boys. I was in that do-as-I-say-not-do-as-I-do grown-up phase. Nonetheless, hurt people hurt people, starting with yourself, and I was truly setting myself up to be hurt.

I became friends with all the regulars at the local bar. After the fiasco with Randall, I felt even more vulnerable and damn right foolish. How could I not know he was married? Again, as I've stated throughout this book, God will not allow you to be a fool forever. He will show you and offer a way out. You just have to want to see and govern yourself accordingly, or as the young folks say, "Stay woke."

I like to say, "stay aware." More about this awareness later.

As I frequent the bar more and more, one of the regulars took a liking to me. I didn't pay him any attention. I just thought of him as a great dance partner. Besides, he was married, and I was still hearted broken over Randall. On several occasions, Jake would ask if he could take me to breakfast after the club closed. I always refused. But one night after dancing, he asked again, and I said, "Sure, why not?" I was famished. I had worked both jobs without getting a chance to eat a good meal.

We met up at the local twenty-four-hour breakfast place a few miles away. There we engage in the per-usual conversation. Then he said it, the indecent proposal—sex! I gasped and said, "No, thank you."

He said, "But you've already said yes. You said yes to breakfast."

My "green" self had no clue that was code for sex. This was my first go around in these streets. I started laughing. As I said before, I laugh when I'm nervous. As he continued to try to convince me to sleep with him, my dysfunctional hurt self began to rationalize his proposal. All the while he was talking and doing some feel-good action to my feet, I was thinking, *What do you have to lose? You already have the scarlet letter M on you. But this time, you can choose to be a mistress, and it can be on your terms.*

I also thought another dysfunctional thought: *You've never had a one-night stand. You've heard of such and wondered what that was like, the power it must possess. This is your opportunity. Hit it and quit it.* That's what they used to say back in my day. *You can do this, Sharon.*

It happened. I became his mistress that night. That one-night stand lasted about three years. It was not my finest moment. There were times I felt bad about it, but most times, honestly, I didn't care. It had been done to me. Other people do it all the time, I rationalized.

But I was not other people. I was supposed to live above that particular sin. Now, mind you, I was fine with the sin of fornication but not adultery—the lies we tell ourselves to justify our actions. Sin is sin. Our culture likes to put sin on a scale. Little sin, big sin. For example, a lie is a little sin; fornication, not little, but not as big as adultery or murder—all the same to God. The Ten Commandments were not written by order of ranking. To me, I see it as a foundation to guide you in this thing called life.

This secret affair, like anything else you do in life, will always come back to hunt and hurt you. And hunt me it did. During the duration of my marriages to Warden 2 and 3, I often wondered if their unfaithfulness to me was karma for what I did. Those thoughts were in my head constantly and *loudly*. So if you're thinking about doing it or doing it again, my advice would be don't. You will eventually marry one day, and even if your partner is faithful, the guilt will get to you, and you will start believing in your mind that you don't deserve an honest marriage because of your sin secret.

Warden Number 2: Stand by Your Man

What generally was a five-minute walk from the law firm to the parking garage felt like infinity. I was praying that I ran into no one that I knew who had seen the morning and/or the prior evening's top news story. I was just a few hundred yards shy of my escape to the elevator when this complete stranger walking toward me felt the need to say, "You are so beautiful."

My escape being unnoticed failed. I thought to myself, *You've got to be kidding me.* I could not possibly look pretty or beautiful because of the night and morning I'd had. I mustered up enough sound to say thank you and prayed she did not see the tears in my eyes that were about to fall. I had the absolute worst forty-eight hours of my life. It was yet again, another bad weekend with Warden number 2. Outbursts were the norm for this angry soul. I was married to an abuser, physical and mental. I don't remember what set off this firestorm, but it ended with police officers at the door. The neighbors had called them. There was no physical abuse this time. He knew better, but that did not stop the police from arresting him.

It was a Saturday, errand and laundry day. I had clothes everywhere in the living room. As the police entered the home, their eyes scanned the room for disturbance. They interviewed us both separately. I advised them that I had not been physically harmed and that the argument just got out of hand. Seeing laundry everywhere, they did not believe me. They assumed my living room was a mess due to a fight. It wasn't. I was not expecting company. My living room looked like a normal room of someone not expecting company. I really think they arrested him because of his prior record of domestic abuse that was in the system. Did I know about this prior record of abuse? Of course I did. It was abuse against me, the first time! We'll get to that story later. In Mississippi, the law is written as such that a statement does not have to come from a victim for an abuser to be arrested. If the officer deems there is probably cause, he/she can arrest an alleged abuser.

With that said, the officer arrested warden number two. I didn't think much of it. I was happy to see him go so I could get a good night's sleep. I got the usual phone call from him an hour later of how sorry he was with the usual tears and how long they were going to keep him. I rolled my eyes and went to sleep.

The next day at church, I and most of the congregation were surprised and treated to the renewal of wedding vows of our bishop and first lady. It was absolutely beautiful. Here I was at church, watching a beautiful ceremony, and my husband was sitting in jail for domestic abuse allegations. My emotions were all over the place. I thought, *What is wrong with me? Why am I in a crazy relationship? I'm a "good girl." I'm thoughtful, fun, beautiful, independent, and faithful. What am I doing wrong?*

These are the common thoughts that ring in the heads of individuals who have been abused in some form or fashion. You think it is your fault that you got picked by this idiot who is disrupting your life. I smiled and tried my best to be happy while watching this beautiful ceremony. It was hard because all I could do was rehearse my problems in my head.

After I arrived home, I received several phone calls from one of my brothers. He was calling for Warden number 2. I was too shameful to say he was in jail. I made up excuses of where he was. That's what we do. We cover for them. He called at least three times. After hearing me lie yet again that the warden was at the store or at a friend's home, I was confronted with words that made me drop the phone. He said, "Well if he is at his friend's home, I guess his twin must be the guy the police arrested for domestic abuse. Have you not seen the news, sis?"

The secret was out for the whole state of Mississippi to see. This was a top news story, not because it was a domestic violence arrest but because he was a state representative. The room started spinning, and I could barely breathe. It was bad enough that the neighbors saw him in handcuffs being placed in the car, but now, the whole state is seeing his picture on the news, and my name has become infamous with the word domestic violence. How was I going to show my face at work tomorrow? How was I going to return to my church? The very thought made me throw up several times throughout the night.

The phone calls from family and "concerned" friends started. I answered none. What would I say? I only had one person to trust in this situation, Ms. Patsy. Ms. Patsy was my mentor at age fourteen. She gave me my first job as a babysitter and took me to a James Robinson crusade where I accepted Christ in my life. She was the only one that could be trusted in a situation like this.

No sleep was had that night. She stayed on the phone with me until four in the morning, praying, encouraging, and keeping me sane. I told her I was not courageous enough to show my face at work, to which she replied, "That is the very thing you need to do, show your face. Nothing happened, right?"

"Yes, ma'am," I replied.

"So go show your face so they can see the evidence for themselves that nothing happened. If you wait even one day, they will assume you're waiting for bruises to fade away and the rumor will only get worse. You don't want that to happen, do you?"

"No, ma'am, I don't."

She was so kind and loving. I'll never forget that act of love shown to me on the darkest night of my life.

As soon as I walked in the office building, the stares began. They got worse when I got to my desk. Everyone—and I mean everyone—came around to "see" my face. It was disguised as, "Hey, girl, I just wanted to come see how you are doing."

These were the fake individuals because they could have just called my extension. They were looking for a damaged woman. But there also were the most concerned ones that came as well. Those are the ones who held my hand and looked me in the eyes and said, "If you need anything—I mean anything—you let me know."

I still remember one individual in particular who, when he said it, I thought, *He is serious. Anything?*

I'll leave that right there. After about three hours of that, I had to get out of there. I could not get any work done, and it was disruptive for the other individuals near me with this constant flow of visitors to our area, all to see little ole me. My supervisor gladly honored my request to leave early. Timing is everything. My exit allowed me to run into the God-sent stranger who told me I was beautiful on the worst day of my life. These are the moments in life that I believe God speaks through strangers to say, "I'm still with you."

I thought I would have peace when I got home to sort all this out and get a nap since I only had two hours of sleep. No, no, no. When I arrived at my home, there were news vans and reporters in front of my home. *What the hell*, I thought to myself. Warden number 2 was scheduled to be released today, and they were waiting for his arrival.

My heart stopped. All I could think about was that my sons would be home from school soon. They had no clue of what transpired over the weekend. It was their weekend with their dad. They missed the drama, this time, that occurred on Saturday night.

As I drove to the driveway, my mama bear instincts kicked in. I was furious. There was no need for the reporter to walk toward me. I was in their face immediately. I shouted, "Are you kidding me? My boys will be home soon. Get off my property. You have no right to be here."

The snappy reporter advised me, with a grin, that they had every right to be there to cover the story. They removed themselves from the grass, but that news van stayed parked on the public street in front of my home.

I called Warden 2, who was at a friend's home. I told him of the chaos he'd caused and that he needed to get these folks from in front of my home. Without missing a beat, he immediately snapped into politician mode and said he was going to speak with a friend, who was also an attorney. The family friend who became our honorary crisis attorney advised us that we should have a press conference so the viewers could see my face and judge for themselves if I had been abused. He also stated that we should do this on our terms or they—the media—would continue to show up at our home or at the state capitol where he worked or even my job at the law firm. To ensure that this would not happen, I reluctantly agreed to a press conference. Our attorney called all the local news station with a verbal press release advising that the representative and his wife would hold a press conference in less than an hour.

The Candidate

He walked through the door as if nothing happened. There was a brief hello, then off to the bedroom he went to find his best suit for the cameras and asked me what I was going to wear. It was clear that this fool, as before, had no real remorse about the situation. It was all about him as usual. There was no time to have a dialogue about our out-of-control marriage with having less than thirty minutes to pull off the front of a perfect couple who had an alleged domestic incident.

I wore my red skirt suit that I still own today. I reapplied my makeup, bumped a few more curls in my hair, and it was showtime. Our attorney had arrived, and so had the media. The three of us stood on that tiny porch to begin the interview. Per our attorney, we agreed that he and Warden 2 would do most of the talking and that I would only answer a few questions if asked. If he felt any questions that were directed toward us was too invasive or out of line, he would interject with an answer.

I stood there nervous while having an out-of-body experience. All I could think about was the bus carrying my teenage boys would be arriving in less than forty minutes. I watched as some neighbors peeked out their windows, while others stood on their porches to watch the shit show.

But not Warden 2. He revelled in the spotlight of the cameras. That's what politicians do! He was ready for his additional fifteen minutes of fame, no matter the cost to me and my boys. I was furious at his calm demeanor and apologetic speech to his constituents, the people of the great state of Mississippi and to his beautiful wife. If I had any food left in my stomach, I think I would have thrown up again and aimed for his shoes.

Done and done, the media circus got their story, and off they went. As soon as we entered the living room and I peeped through the curtain to make sure the media trucks were gone, I told the warden to pack his clothes and get the hell out of the house, something I should have done years earlier. He asked where he was going to go. I told him I didn't care. "Go to a friend. Go to Chicago to visit your family." I did not care. "Just leave, or the media will be back, but a different story will be written about who did what."

It would be a slow news week. My situation was airing on every local network TV station as well as the morning radio talk shows. The callers were brutal with their opinions and comments. One talk show host who is notorious for being opinionated and wrong spoke boldly that I was lying about the alleged abuse and standing by my man. I was furious. But as I listened to his lies and theories and the others who knew nothing about my character, I was also privy to hear some friends call in to defend me. I was crying and smiling all at the same time. If I had the courage I have today, perhaps I would have called in to tell that host where to put his two cents. I was wounded, and the wounded had to take shelter and rest.

There were signs of his unstableness and anger when we first met. I didn't ignore it. I saw it as my cause to help. Also, my thirty-something-year-old self at the time believed his stories that no one believed in him and all of the sorted lies that men tell to women who have nurturing souls. At that age, I had not had enough experience or the expertise to understand who I was dealing with and who I was as a person.

Most women, like myself, are born with a maternal instinct. We are pretty much designed to help, fix, and solve problems. That is why most of us, a time or two, have found a man that need fixing up. We don't intentional go looking for these projects to do. I won't say it just happens. It takes two to start and one to end it. I heard Halle Berry say in an interview once that "if there was a stray dog in town, she was going to find him."

I said, "That's me too!" Once these stray dogs—yes, I said it— find a home in you, they do what untrained dogs do, run loose.

All of the mistakes I've had in my life are totally on me, but there are influencing factors: culture, family, church, and community. All these factors encourage you to trust, forgive, and help. So that is what you do. You trust when you shouldn't. You forgive, and stay instead of forgiving and leaving, you continue to help them while no appreciation is afforded and there is no equal distribution of help. I hope that by sharing my stories with you in this book, you get a quicker sense of when to say *no* and *goodbye* to people who do not have your best interest in mind. In judging to see if you should stay or go, just ask yourself, does this person treat me like person, or do they treat me like an opportunity? One of your answers is in that question.

The only incident of physical abuse happened at our previous home. It happened less than a year of being married to him. I could not believe that I was married to someone who was belligerent and engaged in such reckless behavior of pounding on the countertops or punching the wall during arguments.

After yet another one of his episodes, I'd threaten him with divorce. I was serious this time. I was tired of my boys' seeing his outrageous behavior and covering yet another spot on the wall with artwork to cover up the hole that he'd punch. You must take these abusive bullies seriously. I didn't.

I am, by nature, a fighter. I grew up with three older brothers, so I don't back down from fights. My mistake was that instead of engaging with this person in these verbal fights, I should have been strategically planning my pardon like I did with Warden number 1. You can't tell someone who is enraged with anger that you are leaving them. No, you've got to do it quietly, or you're end up with a punch in the back of the head like me. I was lucky. Yes, I say lucky because some women are not here to tell their story; they are dead. Death from domestic abuse is real. You never think it can happen to you until it does. The National Coalition Against Domestic Violence's (NCADV) website has alarming statistics. Please read and share with any family member you believe to be experiencing any form of abuse.

As I walked away from him to head up the stairs of my condo, he hit me in the back of the head. He hit me so hard that it knocked me out. I don't know how long I was out, but I do remember seeing my deceased grandmother in a vision. It was not my time to go. When I came to, he was kneeling next to me, telling me that he'd called an ambulance, the police, my mom, his mom, my brother, and the church.

As I tried to regain consciousness, I realized what had happened. My eyes immediately scrolled to my boys, who were in the room and saw it all. The guilt still haunts me that I can never erase that memory from their head hurts me the most. The next target of my eyes was the kitchen where the knives were. Every bit of rage rose up in me as I tried to get up to grab a knife. Today, he was going to meet his maker.

He held me down to talk some sense in me. He knew what I wanted to do. He saw my eyes. He said the police were on their way, so there was no need to hurt him. That's the thing about bullies. They don't fight fair. He was a coward. Only cowards sucker punch individuals as they are walking away. Never turn your back on some-one you're verbally fighting with. Always exit the area walking back-ward. I would be diagnosis with a concussion that would plague me with short-term and long-term memory losses.

Counseling

I would like to tell you I left him, but no one encouraged me to do so except my two boys. They were not afraid of him. He never was abusive to them. They were afraid he would hurt me, all the yelling and arguments that should not have been had. My brother, who picked me up from the hospital, said nothing that I expected him to say. I expected him to say, "You want his legs or his arms broken?" But he did not.

I wanted him to say, "We have your back. You don't have to deal with this alone." But I was alone.

What he did say surprised me and had me thinking he must be an abuser too. He just folded his arms and said, "It's your choice to stay with him if you want." That was our talk. It was nothing.

The church called to check on me. It was the same advice as my brother but with a twist. The advice was not "it's your choice to stay with him" but that I should stay with him and go to counseling with another couple who has gone through what we've experienced. I want to be very clear. I blame no one but myself for my dating and staying married to a man with anger issues. I just write what I experienced so that some young lady or young man who is in an abusive situation can run and not walk away from these toxic relationships. Did counseling help? Well, what counseling? I never got a call from the experienced couple. I felt like it was all swept under a rug. My thoughts. My experience.

Seasonal Help

As Warden number 2 and I moved forward in our relationship—my project—I worked hard to help him get elected to the house of representatives for our state. He was a good-looking man with intelligence to match, just not one ounce of common sense. There, I said it. But that didn't stop the political groupies from gathering around him at events and even at church.

There are those individuals who want to replace you in your relationship with your spouse and/or significant other. Be it by the actions of your spouse or significant other or the pure boldness of an individual who has an unrealistic view that they can do your job better. These individuals watch you from afar and say, "I should be his wife," or "I should be her husband." "They"—meaning us—don't deserve "them," our spouse. They have not one clue what it takes to be you in that 24-7 365-day-a-year relationship, yet they are so eager to step in to "do it right." Delusional minds often tickle me. They just want the spotlight you're standing in.

This brings to mind when I was married to Warden number 2, the politician. Political spouses, in the minds of some and themselves, are the local celebrities. Politicians always have individuals who have crushes on them, and they think they are the Barack Obama or Jack Kennedy of our city. You know, they walk and talk with that political swagger.

This particular scene happened one day after church. Yes, church. Don't be fooled by the cover title "Christian." Some of these women will go after your man like any other woman and swear that God told them too. I always saw this one particular young lady talking to Warden number 2 every Sunday. In the beginning it didn't bother me. We were at church! Surely, she was not flirting with him. They are just talking about the word for today, or she's asking him something about politics. I felt my superior looks were better than hers, but we all know, looks have nothing to do with infidelity. "There's nothing to worry about there, Sharon," I told myself.

Well, the after church miniconversations continued happening almost every Sunday like clockwork. After several occasions, my mind recognized her flirtatious hand on his shoulder, his smile to her and her minilaughs with him. I thought, *What is so damn funny every week?*

Every now and then, I would mention to him that I saw his little girlfriend all up next to him again after church, to which he would smile and wave it off as her just being nice. I told him to handle her, or I would.

Well, she did her per-usual after-church being all up in his face, and I assumed he said something to her about my talk with him because she decided to grace me with her presence on that day. She had no clue what she was about to get. I guess this was her attempt to throw me off. She approached me with the wicked and deceiving smile. "Sharon, how are you, first lady?"

"Very well. Thank you for asking." Y'all know in my head I was saying a lot more, but we were in the church parking lot, so technically, still on church grounds, and I had to behave.

She proceeded. "Are y'all going to the political dinner next week?"

"Yes, of course we are. It's mandated to go to all these chicken dinners."

"Well, does Erik have any single political friends that you can set me up with?"

As I stared her wicked eyes down, I said the following: "You can go with Erik. As a matter of fact, you can go to all these engagements with him, and you can wash his dirty underwear and cook his food. What time would you like for me to drop him off and what is your address?" I really wanted her to say "Yes, I'll take him," because my pardon was way overdue. But she didn't. She didn't want my full time job as wife. She just wanted the light I stood in.

Yes, all that came out before I knew it. It had been building up for months, and this heifer had the nerve to come stare me in the face and basically ask for him, but in the form of, "Does he have a friend who has his job and going to the same event he's going to?"

I thought, *You couldn't have asked him this question while you were over there grinning in his face?* Yes, she could have. I'm assuming her strategy was to come give me a few minutes of her smiles and giggles to throw me off the scent of her trying to set something in motion with my spouse.

Ladies, just a freebie here from a former spouse: never doubt that the wife does not know what you are doing. Remember, she was once single like you and may have done what you're doing but did it much better. As some would say, game recognizes game.

She tilted her whole body back in shock. She did not see that coming. She laughed it off and told me I was funny. My eyes told her something different.

She still continued to get in his face after church but less frequently and with less touching and smiles. She knew I had my eye on her. He never confessed to anything until my mom's funeral, almost fifteen years later. She was there, and he brought it up. The strangest thing: I hadn't given it a second thought. We were divorced. He's remarried, and I'm there with Warden number 3, and he feels this is the perfect time to confirm to me that yes, she crossed the line when we were married. I just looked at him with my eyes that said I really didn't give a damn back then and certainly not now. My conversation with her back fifteen years prior was solely to explain to her that if you want him, you get all of him. Don't apply for seasonal work when you can get the job full-time and all the benefits and stress that come with it.

Ah, the seasonal help. Let's dive right in. When a company requires additional workforce for its peak season, they hire seasonal workers. Of course, I googled "seasonal worker!" It stated the following: "Employment that does not continue year-round but usually recurs." The following was stated regarding benefits: "Oftentimes full-time and some part-time employees get access to best compensation and benefits, but temporary and seasonal employees are left out." Allow that to sink in seasonal workers. You get no benefits.

So what equates to peak season in your spouse's life that would prompt them to cheat on you and hire seasonal help? *Ego* and a rebellious spirit. These wardens prey on individuals who can and willingly be used. The seasonal help has arrived to boost the warden's ego during his peak season. Only one problem: she or he has been hired without any said notice to the comanager, the other spouse. Seasonal workers are not a constant, just someone that recurs periodically. I'm not here judging. I can't. I've had my twist as seasonal helper. I just remember when I became woke about being seasonal help and placed value on myself; that position was no longer an option for me. I remember it like yesterday.

Happy New Year

We sat on the back porch of the rental home to discuss our foresee-able divorce. I wanted out. I'd had enough with Warden number 2. It was very clear that he was not going to change his ways. I had stayed for three more years since the moment he made me infamous. I had not been courageous enough to pardon myself. My boys were older, beginning high school, and I'd just given birth to our son. I felt in my spirit that my boys would not let this man live if he laid another hand on me in error of judgment. I also felt the same way.

As we sat outside to ring in the new year with champagne and stogies, I told him that our child could have a great upbringing with two parents living separately, or our son could visit one in jail and the other at the cemetery and that I did not mind being arrested.

He stared at me for the longest. I sat there waiting for him to respond via narrative or action. I was ready. For all the verbal bully-ing that continued, I knew one thing for sure, he was not going to lay another hand on me. After the first incident, he never slept peaceful lying next to me ever again. He knew at any time, I could, if I wanted to, get revenge.

Also, in Mississippi, there is a three-strike rule when it comes to domestic violence. The first two arrests were just considered mis-demeanors with a twenty-four-to-forty-eight-hour stay in jail. Your third offense would get you five to ten years in jail, and it would be a felony on your record. Bullies are crazy, but they ain't that crazy. They know when to act up and when to straighten up. You just have to stand up to them and eventually pardon yourself from their presence. I did just that. Life was grand again.

> Accountability: the quality or state of being accountable especially; an obligation or willing-ness to accept responsibility or to account for one's actions.

The failing marriage belongs to both parties. It doesn't mat-ter if it is fifty/fifty, sixty/forty, seventy/thirty, or even ninety-five/

five; it all adds up to one-hundred-percent failure. Reflecting back on all three of my marriages, part of my contribution was not being honest with myself and my needs. I put the power of being nurtured, encouraged, and protected solely in the hands of the wardens. That's what I was incorrectly taught. That's what I saw in my culture. Although this was the warden's just duty, the backup source—me—should have always been ready to restore power. My power, should my main source stop working, should have activated itself. Let's use the following analogy of electricity in the home to illustrate what should have taken place.

The electricity in the home works properly, correct? But if a storm comes through, the power sometimes fails. What happens next? Well, if you're unprepared, you sit in a dark house and wait for help to come fix it for your family. Or if you've prepared yourself for such an event, you go to your garage or storage and you crank up the generator for power. Now this generator is not intended to replace the original source of energy; it is just the for the stormy seasons on an as-needed basis. This is true with marriages. You are not to replace your spouse's duties, but you exist for times of low power and/or outages!

We all have marital storms just like we have weather related storms. When the main power is out in your relationship due to a storm, what are your options? If the power of both parties is absent or operate at a very low percentage, what are your options? When there is no backup generator per se, said parties will sit in darkness (figuratively and literally) until help arrives (counseling), or in some instances, fumble their way through the dark, trying all sorts of ways to provide energy back into the dwelling.

Unfortunately, these sources of energy are short-term and may cause more interruption than help. Darkness also produces fear, fear of the unknown. The questions of when, how, and who are a constant in your head. When will our power return? How did this happen? Whose fault is it? I don't know about you, but oftentimes when I've lost power at my home or relationship due to a storm or an accident, I'm mindful of what I took for granted when it was available, and I'm certainly more grateful when it returns to normal.

For some couples, that is the case in their marriage. They recover, and they are stronger and more appreciative than they've ever been in their journey. But for some, they see it as an opportunity to do things in the dark that they believe goes unnoticed. Even in the dark, most of us can feel movement or hear footsteps. When one sense cannot perform at its maximum capacity, then the other senses step into play with highest alerts. DEFCON, if you will.

No matter how strong your foundation is, you are not exempt from or immune to a storm. What couples should do is be storm prepared.

On the American Red Cross website, for emergency, they suggest that you make a plan, which consists of creating and practicing an emergency plan so your family will know what to do in a crisis. Here is what they suggest you should do in three easy steps:

1. With your family or household members, discuss how to prepare and respond to the types of emergencies that are most likely to happen where you live, learn, work, and play.
2. Identify responsibilities for each member of your household and how you will work together as a team.
3. Practice as many elements of your plan as possible.

Marriages would last much longer if plans were discussed frequently regarding preexisting conditions or plans in the event of an emergency or a catastrophe. The American Red Cross identifies twenty-two different types of emergencies: chemical emergency, drought, earthquake, fire, flood, flu, food safety, heat wave, highway safety, hurricane, landslide, nuclear explosion, poisoning, power outage, terrorism, thunderstorm, tornado, tsunami, volcano, water safety, wildfire, and winter storm. Well, if that don't say it all, I don't know what does. Just as the American Red Cross identifies twenty-two types of emergencies, so it is with marriages. There are no two couples with the same problems. Generally, yes, but not specifically. So the relief must be unique to make whole the situation. Your marriage is not your brother's or your neighbor's. It is yours alone.

This DEFCON power you possess, honestly, what do you do with it? You've read my stories in the previous chapters. Sometimes I fought. Sometimes I shut down. Sometimes I waited to be paid for my inconvenience. When I fought, I fought the wrong way. You know the per usual, verbal and/or physical. I did not have a strategy. I did not have an endgame, whether good or bad. I just fought.

If you don't plan your life, someone else will. Recover, forgive, and find your purpose.

CHAPTER 4

Why We Stay

Shame

"Hey, Shannon," she said as I answered my phone.

For privacy's sake, we'll call her Mary. I replied, "Mary, this is Sharon, not Shannon.

She began with, "I'm so sorry. I was trying to call another person and got you instead."

I didn't believe that story at all. I don't believe in random and because she also stated that she and another person were just talking about me the other day. No doubt she'd heard the news I was divorced, but nonetheless, she had to ask for herself. "How's your husband?"

Like I mentioned in another chapter, these individuals care nothing for me because if they did, they would follow protocol and at least ask how I'm doing first, especially knowing I lost my mother less than a year prior. No, they only cared about one thing and one thing only: gossip. They go straight for the main course and ask about Warden number 3. Again, just to confirm the rumor, not that they cared how he's doing. She's never asked before; why ask now?

At that time, I was very comfortable telling folks I was now divorced. It rolled off my tongue like fine wine. I confirmed to her I was divorced. Her prompt response caught me a little off guard but not shocking enough where it would startle me. She said, "Girl, my mother use to say women like you can't keep a man."

Yes, ma'am; yes sir, she said that to me. If she would have said that to me a year prior, I probably would have burst into tears. But she caught me all healed up. I just held my peace. But in my head, I was saying, *And homely women like you can't get a man.*

She'd, herself, had been divorced for over twenty years with no prospects that were had or have been seen by the masses. I wanted to say it to her, but I didn't. I still have to answer to God for what I say. He ain't finished with me yet.

This is one of the main reasons women and men stay in non-confirming relationships, because of people like her who have toxic mouths. She had no right to say that to me. She could think it. She could even discuss my situation with others, which I believe she did, but she had no right to put me down like that. But that is the nature of people. They get a little information, and they feel they have the right to diagnose your life.

There's an old saying: "Tell the truth and shame the devil." There are those who would have you believe that there is shame in getting a divorce. That is why most people continue to stay in worthless marriages or long-term relationships only to be abused and cheated on. My friend, you are the most courageous person standing in the room if you've had to get a divorce for the first, second, or even third time. You tried, and that is all that matters. There are those who want to shame you because they don't have your courage, and as long as you stay in the same boat as they are in—the unhappy boat, not the love boat—you put them in an uncomfortable position. Courage.

When you divorce, the secrets are out. What's done in the dark comes to light. Oh, the devil doesn't like that. That is why he and your spouse would rather you stay silent and be a good little mate and not disturb the waters. My friend, you were made to disturb the waters. Bad things happen when good people do nothing. That can be said in the marriage realm as well. You were created to thrive. God never said, "Marry and allow anything to happen to you." No, He created you for a purpose. If you are beaten down with physical, emotional, and/or mental abuse, how can you serve His kingdom? If you're not honest with yourself, how can you be honest with anyone you come in contact with. You have to own yourself. Shame the devil and tell the truth. The truth will correct, or the truth will get gone those who do not have your best interest at heart.

You remember John 8:1–11, the scripture relating to the adulterous woman. They only brought the woman from this two-person act of sin. Shame has always been forced on the women. Nothing has changed in modern times. When people hear you, a woman, are divorced, they immediately want to know what's wrong with you. Oh, and don't let this be your second or third divorce; you for certain, are dammed to be. On the other hand, if a man is divorced, pity is bestowed on him.

I'm writing this book for everyone, men and women, but come on, men! You know we women get more judgment than you do. If we marry an older man, it is said that we are gold diggers, and he's our sugar daddy. But the man who marries a younger woman is praised, complimented, and patted on the back. "You ole dog," is said as a compliment. Stop shaming people! Shame will make you stay!

Children's Sake

No decent human being wants to split up a family, but circumstances are sometimes beyond our control. During and/or after the separation, invisible lines will be drawn, either by spouses or by the children on their own accord or with coaching of a parent. Usually, the absentee parent plays on the sympathy of the children with untruths, and the parent with custody becomes public enemy number 1. Children inadvertently choose sides based on what they see and the limited data they are being given.

In my case, as a child in the early 1970s, Mom and Dad were split up by the time I was two. I don't remember hearing anything bad about my dad, just that he and Mom were separated and not divorce. I remember Mom's having boyfriends, and we were not allowed to see my pops. I didn't know why. Those were the days where grown folks kept grown folks' business to themselves.

Dad thought he could outsmart Mom and rented a house on the same street where we lived when I was seven or so. We were not allowed to go to Dad's home. We were given strict instructions not to go and given a speech of what would happen if we did. Mom even solicited the grandmas of the neighborhood to keep watch when she was not at home. Those were the days where everyone on your block truly knew each other, and family really did look after each other.

Luckily for us, Dad's home was on the same side of the street as ours, and there were no fences. We would sneak down to Dad's home to visit and get something great to eat. We were poor, very poor. Food was scarce. We didn't mind the risk of getting a beating if Mama found out. The reward was a food: greens and corn bread, rice pudding, smothered and fried chicken, soda pop, and some good ole Maxwell House coffee. Daddy always had a pot percolating.

I remember sitting on the side steps of my dad's home, enjoying a delicious meal when out of the side of my eye, I saw a green Thunderbird make its way down the street. I dropped everything and took off running. It was Mama!

My dad made fun of me about that day many times. He said all he saw was dust. He said I ran so fast, he thought I turned into a ghost.

Eventually, Mom and Dad worked things out, and we freely visited Daddy. I would learn later that the issue was child support. I would learn much later by watching the Hulu series *Mrs. America* that there was no law for a man to pay child support in the early 1970s. As I watched that episode, I thought of Mama. I had no idea. I silently asked her spirit to forgive me because I, as a child, made her feel guilty for not staying with my dad and keep us away from him. Just like any child, you don't know what each parent is dealing with in a divorce or a separation. You have to reconcile that the best decisions are being made for two adults who can't work things out, especially if you are unharmed, clothed, have shelter, and have enough food to survive another day. It wasn't until after Mama's death that I found a copy of an old claim form that she submitted trying to get VA benefits. I read the following, and it broke my heart. I whispered again to her spirit "I'm sorry, Mama."

In Her Own Words

1. The Veteran was physically abusive to me on every instance that we were separated. 1963 or 1964 we separated for the first time in Edwards, MS. Separated again in 1964 in Jackson, MS. In 1966 we separated again. In 1969 we separated again. He was always beating and tried to kill me with a pipe. We separated at least 5 or 6 times so I could survive.

2. I tried again and again to live together with the veteran but it seemed that his abuse of me physically and my children emotionally and psychologically was progressively getting worse as time went by.

3. Me and my husband attempted to live together but it seemed that he was bent on destroying me. We went to legal services and they encouraged us to stay together for the children sake to try to work things out.

4. The veteran did send a check monthly for the support of his children but never for me. The VA sent an apportionment of $10 then $15 but never got higher than $20 monthly. He never willingly of his own accord sent money to support his children and me.

5. When we first married, we lied in Edwards, MS from 1961 to 1964. In 1964 we moved to Jackson. Our last separation was in Jackson was 1975. We never officially divorced and never even applied for divorce.

These are the words of my precious mom that I found in one of her purses later after her death. She was filing a claim with the VA for benefits that she should have received. But to no avail did she receive anything. I thought to myself, *Why would she hold on to this claim form that is several decades old?* The words "we hold these truths to be self-evident" rain in my head. I cried even more for her experience and the ghost that would haunt her years later of never receiving help in the raising of her children. Yet she held on to a piece of paper that spoke beyond her death of her experience.

I've had a few episodes with my sons as well postdivorce. It takes a toll on the children. They say things to you during this season that rip your heart apart or have episodes of outburst that are not the norm. I remember after my first divorce, one of my sons walked up to me, all of his five-year-old self, and proclaimed he wanted to stay with his father. In shock, I counted to ten to compose myself and keep from crying. Then I marched him to his room and pulled out his little kid's suitcase and asked what he wanted to take with him. The look on his face said it all. He didn't want to leave his mama. That was his way of letting me know he did not like the situation. He never brought that request up again. Children will make you stay!

Finances, Debt, Lifestyle

I recently learned of a friend who just purchased a new home with his estranged wife. They separated for almost two years. He was a cheater, and she found out, but here we are two years later with them purchasing a bigger home—not just any home, a very expensive home. In some sick way, people do tie themselves up in bills to stay together. They don't actual commit to each other; they commit to something in common. The kids, the cars, the house, the family vacations—all fake, all miserable, and all become cheaters. He'll cheat again, and she'll get another anonymous letter, text, or e-mail again regarding same. It happened before, it will happen again.

He hates that she posts family pics on social media, and every time I've spoken with him, he's downplayed their relationship and states repeatedly that he's there for his children. This is not a marriage; this is a business arrangement. I recommend not making any new bills until you sort out if you are going to pardon yourself or not. For whatever reason, if a new bill is created, somewhere deep inside, you have made an unconscious decision to stay. The bill has committed you two to stay together at least eighteen to forty-eight more months. It's crazy to think this action exists, but it happens all the time, and I can say as a witness, it happened with me. Making new bills makes you stay.

Courage

It was a casual call; well, so I thought. Her voice was low, and I could hear concern in her tone. "Hey," she said.

I said hello. She said, "Well, I want to get your opinion because you're strong and kind of an expert."

In my mind, I was thinking, *Cool. Shoot. Yes, I know a few good things. Give me what you got.*

The next few sentences that came from her did not shock me but did catch me off guard. She said, "He's asked for a divorce for the third time."

I immediately wanted to say, "Damn, give his ass what he wants. It's not like you don't know he's cheating on you." But you can't say that at a very sensitive moment like this. Your job is to listen. Although she was asking for advice, she didn't really want it. She just really wanted someone to listen who would not be judgmental. Well, who better than me to not be judgmental since I recently filed for divorce number three myself. I was certainly in no position to judge. That's when it hit me regarding the reference "you're an expert." Although it was an accurate statement, wearing the scarlet letter D for the third time was no fun.

No matter what, you are judged by family, friends, society, and more shockingly, by yourself. As I continued to listen to her, I'm thinking (well, really judging), *Why in the hell won't she leave his sorry ass?* Immediately, my mind was quickened. Whatever you say in your head, you hear it loud and clear in your heart.

As soon as I thought it, my spirit said, "Yeah, and look how long it took you to get that third divorce. What were you waiting on?"

That's when I remember her also saying, "Because you are strong." What my friend needed now was a lesson in being strong and gaining some courage. From that moment forward, I did my best to intently listen before I uttered any words. Pause when needed to pause and really listen since she made the phone call to me and not the other way around. This new journey that I'm on has allowed me to give pauses in conversations. I'm so excited about this new behavior of mine, listening.

I've always stated to people when called for advice, XYZ happened to me, and I did XYZ to remedy the situation. I always remind them that every situation is different, and I will never tell you what to do. I cannot advise you on what to do based on your side of the story. There are always three sides to every story: his, hers, and the truth. I recommend two things: if you're not in any harm's way, go to counseling if you think that will help and make a pro and con list of why you should stay and/or why you should pardon yourself. Lack of courage will make you stay!

Marriage Club

Like in the animal kingdom where many herds group together, so it is with humans. Athletes, religious affiliates, actors, single people, and (oh, yes) married folks—all of these are unofficial clubs that we belong too, some by default and some by choice. When you are married, you do married things such as double date, take trips together, raise children in similar environments, go to sporting events and concerts just to name a few.

If you try to break from the unofficial club through divorce, you are considered an outcast. You don't get invitations to any events as you did predivorce. During your divorce consideration period, you are encouraged to stay together, not because it is good for you or your spouse to press forward. No, staying together is for the couple who also has a damaged relationship that if one more thing happen, their marriage is over. Thus, your making a move, having the courage to break free, could set a domino effect that causes disruption to an already disruptive setting.

Trust me, that couple that you are trying to save by staying married will do one of the following: they will get a divorce without your permission and shrug their shoulders as if y'all did not make a pact to not divorce, or they will come to an amicable agreement with their spouse where they live under the same roof as "partners" because of finances or appearances or other unknown reasons. They will live out secret agent lifestyles. They've agreed to allow the other person to do whatever they want.

But is that not divorce? Some people just want roommates at any cost, and if truth be told, they just want to continue in the dysfunction that has embedded in their lives. And for some, this setting of still being married but free allows that person to use any third party that enters the relationship. They will use the "I'm married, so I can't commit to you" line. That is, in itself, the original problem, not committing. The club will make you stay!

Fear

I had stopped talking to her, which is not my character with friends. In the beginning, we had a great relationship, but she betrayed my confidence with information I provided to her. I don't do betrayal. So when my phone rang at four in the morning, all sort of thoughts went through my head. First thought of course, *What the hell does she want?* Then it proceeded with, *Is there something wrong with her family?* And finally, and no I'm not proud of this one, *Did she win the lottery?* Heck, I better answer this call just in case.

It was another one of Mega Millions big drawings, and as I checked the news feed to see if there was a winner in between her multiple calls, the news feed showed the jackpot back at the beginning amount of forty million. So yes, honey, I answered that call on her third attempt.

What I did not expect to hear on the other side of the phone was the call of a physically abused woman. Her voice was filled with fear, dismay, and anger as she began to detail every moment of her last twenty-four hours. I felt helpless and a rush of emotions ran through my soul. I hated him, her husband, for what he did to her. This is absolutely not the time to say I told you so or anything of that matter. It is just time to listen. Being very careful not to offer advice and my two cents as I had previously when we were speaking, I told her that I would pray for her soul and strength for her body and that she should keep herself safe. I was not going to tell her to leave him.

After all, I didn't leave my abuser immediately. It would be three more years before I would have the courage to pardon myself from that toxic relationship.

Later that day, she called again. This time, I did not pick up. I don't know what it was that gave me that resistance to not pick up the phone. Was it not wanting to relive my moments of abuse if I heard her words? Was it a sense of feeling betrayed again by her if I spoke against him and she uses it in their next fight? Or was it maybe just not enough strength to deal with her problem when I had so many going on myself?

Whatever it was, it was wrong of me not to pick up. After I did not answer her call, she texted. She wanted me to know she was at the doctor's office because she feared she had broken ribs and a concussion. It all came flooding back to me. I did not have a broken rib, but I did suffer a concussion from a blindsided blow to the back of my head as I walked away from an argument with my ex.

I immediately called her. In this moment of shock that someone just abused you, there are very few people you want to talk to. So I knew I had to return her call. You're not thinking rationally in this moment. You feel shame that you allowed this to happen to you. You're not even sure yet if you're going to leave him. You don't even realize you are a victim. You are living in a realm of time that does not exist to anyone else but you, playing over and over again in your mind.

I still withheld on giving advice. I just wanted her to know she was cared for and that she would survive this episode in her life like I did. I shared with her that I was reading *The Daily Stoic* and that it was helping me in my season of unfortunate events. My final words to her was that I hope she would allow God to guide her on her journey as she began the healing process. I don't know why she decided not to *pardon* herself, but she didn't and hasn't as of the writing of this book. Fear will make you stay!

Religion

We'd just finished midday Bible study. "Hey, Sharon, how are you?"

"I'm well. How about yourself?"

"Doing well also. I've been following you on Facebook and saw your wedding photos," she said with a smile.

I didn't want to break her heart, but I had to and do it quick. Now that I was back at church, it would not take long for the word to spread that I was divorced again. I wanted her to hear it first from me. So as gently and sternly as I could, I declared that I was divorced. And on cue, there was that look that one gets when telling another party you are divorced. I took a deep breath and waited for the following question of what happened. I tried to be as general as possible because no matter what I said, she was going to have a religious point of view. Not her fault; that's just church folk behavior. There is this one-size-fits-all mentality.

We stood talking, and before I knew it, we were sitting, and that meant only one thing: an impromptu counseling session. My dear church member meant well, and every thought and advice were received in love. But again, she was attempting to diagnosis the death of my marriage by the few things I was saying. And of course, the old "you need to wait on God" was said.

I wanted to say, "I waited many years before I tried again." I waited, per the unwritten church rules. There are just men in sheep's clothing who will say and do anything to get you but not keep you. But I didn't. However, I did proclaim to her that wait time had nothing to do with it. The warden had a rebellious spirit, and I knew it. I just didn't calculate that he would use it on and against me. I knew she meant well.

She proclaimed that our living apart was the culprit. I told her I disagreed. The warden and I saw each other almost daily. There are many happy marriages with spouses living in different cities, states, and/or country. There are jobs that take one spouse out of town frequently such as truck drives, military, entertainers, just to name a few. I knew the following sentence would flow from here soon. Divorce is not an option for my family. I told her I could appreciate her thought process and what a noble position to have. But the same Bible we read does state the following:

> For the woman who has a husband is bound by the law to her husband as long as he lives. But if the husband dies, she is released from the law of her husband. So then if, while her husband lives, she marries another man, she will be called an adulteress; but if her husband dies, she is free from the law, so that she is no adulteress, though she has married another man. Therefore, my brethren, you also have become dead to the law through the body of Christ, that you may be married to another—to Him who was raised from the dead, that we should bear fruit to God. (Romans 7:2–4)

Many have confused the scripture above for their own benefit like my friend. Bless her heart. We all know that reading the Bible can sometimes be complicated. And other times, as simple as ABCs and 123s. Does death in the scripture above mean physical death only? Could it be that emotional or spiritual death as well? We all know that Christ spoke in parable to help those to understand who had agendas. I totally agree with Christ's method. Some people are so "religious" that they have a warped understanding of the scriptures. Let's take a look at Roman 8:6–7:

> For to be carnally minded is death, but to be spiritually minded is life and peace. Because the carnal mind is enmity against God; for it is not subject to the law of God, nor indeed can be.

So let's clear the air. If your spouse is cheating, (1) he is dead to you because the scriptures say so (to be carnally minded), and (2) that person is not subject to the law of God. So for every person telling a woman she has to stay with a man even though he is cheating on her, abusive to her, whether physically or mentally, I say check your scriptures again and leave your egos and traditions at the door.

I don't find it random that Jesus met the woman who've had five husbands at a well—a well, a place to be refreshed and replenished. It was an appointed time. The Scriptures did not identify why or how she had five husbands. Jesus did not judge her regarding her marriages, only her shacking up! He knew that men used women, and just like today, women were coming up dead because the men did not want a divorce because that meant making the woman whole again (finances). It's always about the money! Jesus talked with this woman because she was strong and courageous. Religion did not make her stay!

CHAPTER 5

Redemption

Before we discuss the post-pardon season, let's talk about redemption. *Redemption* can be defined as "the action of saving or being saved from sin, error, or evil and the action of regaining or gaining possession of something in exchange for payment or clearing a debt.

Clearing a debt—let's begin here.

Have you ever felt like you were or are being punished in your marriage? You're trying to figure out what you've done wrong to make your spouse turn against you. For whatever reason, you are public enemy number one. Instead of enjoying a blissful and purposeful relationship, you are being punished daily, weekly, monthly, and/or yearly for a or several offenses that you have no idea you've committed and/or have not been pardoned for.

If you have been advised of your offenses against the marriage and you have gone through the rehabilitation process, your said partner is supposed to reconcile with you and not make you pay for your offenses forever. It's called forgiveness.

Forgiving someone does not mean you have to forget what happened. You're only human. But if that person has been rehabilitated, then your just duty, by God's law, is to live peaceably with them. You are not to hold them in the prison of a marriage or relationship if you are unwilling to forgive. If you hold grudges, that means that you have not granted your spouse a full or an absolute pardon. You've only granted a partial pardon. That's not fair.

Repay no one evil for evil. Have regard for good things in the sight of all men. If it is possible, as much as depends on you, live peaceably with all men. (Romans 12:18)

Review the following and be honest about your actions when it comes to pardoning.

There are four types of pardons:

- Full—unconditionally absolves the person of the conviction and all of the crime's consequences
- Partial—only relieves the person from some of the crime's punishment or consequences
- Absolute—granted without any conditions
- Conditional—some condition, usually to be fulfilled by the person seeking the pardon must occur before the pardon takes effect. Some conditional pardons become void when a specified condition occurs, such as the former offender committing another crime

We've all been granted one or all four of the pardons above in our relationships over our lifetime. When the wrong pardon is applied, devastating events may occur. Recovery can be had if hearts are willing. But matters of the heart are delicate. Some fare well in the mending of the hearts and some not so much.

A conditional pardon is allowed to begin with before granting full and absolute pardons because some will take advantage of your kindness mistaking it for weakness when you pardon them for offenses. When this occurs, you have the right to void their pardon.

If you've served your time, exhibited good behavior, and are genuinely regretful for your offenses and your spouse *refuses* to pardon you, you will have to pardon yourself! Or if you are the spouse who has given many pardons and the offender *refuses* to abide by the marital laws, you can pardon yourself! You do not have to serve a life sentence of misery.

My number one movie of all time is *Shawshank Redemption*. I'm sure I've watched that movie a hundredth time and counting. The storyline flows easily and it has a happy ending. But the many scenes before the happy ending are hard to watch. Such as life.

If you've seen this movie, you are getting an aha moment right now regarding your current or former experience regarding a relationship. For the rest, watch the movie!

Perhaps calling my ex-husband's wardens had to do with the character of Andy Dufresne's relationship with warden Norton. The warden had an opportunist relationship with Andy. Andy was his prisoner for life!

Andy committed no crime that was worthy of the two life sentences he received. Nonetheless, there he was in a conundrum. He suffered and lost nineteen years of his life in the Shawshank prison. He knew he did not belong there but there was nothing he could do about it, until.

After you've suffered a while, God can and will rescue you. But you've got to be prepared.

After seventeen years in prison, Andy is brought the news he's been waiting to hear. There is proof that he is innocent. Knowing it was the right thing to do to pardon Andy, Warden Norton was not having it. Instead, he doubles down on Andy with punishment by locking him in solitary confinement away from his friends and made many threats. Sounds familiar? Have you been threatened and/or kept away from family and friends by your warden?

Just like us, Andy is contemplating his options with haste. How to pardon his own self since the warden is unwilling. He always had a plan to leave, but like us, was slow-moving in executing this plan until now. He kept the warden happy for another year for the sake of his own life and benefits to his friends he loved so dearly.

The most powerful and my favorite part in the movie *Shawshank Redemption* is the "Get busy living or get busy dying" scene. So intense. Despair and hope wrapped tight like a burrito for this scene.

A cryptic conversation is had between friends. Andy, like us, reflects on what has brought him to this point in his life and the storms he had to endure. Then he talks about a future outside the institution of the prison. He is hopeful. His friend Red, like some folks who have been institutionalized by marriage, cannot see their lives any other way but the way it is currently.

Everyone thinks you are crazy because you've come up with a plan for a new life. They don't believe you will do it or can do it. But the twins of pressure and time speak a different story. When it is time to go, you'll know it.

When you pardon yourself, it won't be pretty as you will learn of my experience in the next chapter. And just like Andy, you may have to crawl through five hundred yards of sewage, figuratively, to be free.

When Andy made it outside the prison, he cried and raise his hands to the Lord. That's exactly what I did on my resurrection day I spoke of earlier.

After Andy left, the following is a narrative from Red—an unforgettable dialogue.

> Some birds aren't meant to be caged. Their feathers are just too bright. And when they fly away, the part of you that knows it was a sin to lock them up does rejoice. But still the place you live in is that much more drab and empty that they are gone. I guess I just miss my friend.

As stated previously, this book is not advocating divorce. On the contrary, I'm hoping that the transparency of my experience will restore relationships. But we know that not all relationships can, or should I say, will be restored to their original form.

Pardon is an exemption from punishment. If you do not pardon yourself or the other person on time, you or they will (and most reading this know this to be true) exhibit the dysfunctional behaviors that I wrote about. You alone or the both of you will become as carnal-minded as one can be because you feel broken, damaged, used, and misunderstood.

I was very transparent with you and shared my history of all the foolish behavior I participated in during my post pardon seasons after wardens 1 and 2. Welp! Thank God for my resurrection on May 5 after warden 3. God gave me a second touch! He had just rescued me from a dysfunctional life and gave me another opportunity, like Andy, to actually live and not simply exist. No way was I going to mess up my new beginning by getting back in those streets living a carnal lifestyle. No, I was on the other side now—peace, joy, gratefulness, no more cloudy days crying, and no more cloudy days drinking.

But deciding to live a peaceful life does not mean disruptions won't come. Plus, there's this thing called memory. You forgive but you don't forget. And sometimes people don't let you forget so you can heal. The post-pardon (post-divorce) season that you find yourself in or will find yourself in, is a grey area that can make you feel you are on a roller coaster. No one, not me or your mama can tell you how to handle it. But you will find your way. Chapter 5, "Post Pardon," is written to give you a little insight into what I experienced in my last post-pardon season. You may have similar experiences. Sometimes you're going to feel like the season is getting worse before it getting better. But it does get better.

CHAPTER 6

$\sim$

Postpardon

Stages 1, 2, 3

The Mayo Clinic describes the emotions of a mother's delivery of a baby (postpartum) as excitement, joy, fear, anxiety, and depression. The same can be said for your postpardon (after divorce) state of mind, along with a few more emotions such as anger, bitterness, and resentment. The Mayo Clinic also advises the following, and I agree:

> Postpartum depression isn't a character flaw or weakness. Sometimes it's simply a complication of giving birth. If you have postpartum depression, prompt treatment can help you manage your symptoms and help you bond with your baby.

Do you not realize that you are giving birth to your new self or in the alternative, rebirth of the former you after a divorce? There are three stages of childbirth delivery. With that said, we shall correlate three stages for postpartum and postpardon and hopefully prompt you to treatment to manage the emotions you are dealing with.

There are eight primary emotions that are identified by Robert Plutchik. At any time, with other influences, these emotions can spin off of other ranges. These eight basic emotions are:

1. Fear: feeling of being afraid, frightened, scared (terror; apprehension)
2. Anger: feeling angry. (rage; annoyance)
3. Sadness: feeling sad. (grief; pensiveness)
4. Joy: feeling happy (ecstasy; serenity)
5. Disgust: feeling something is wrong (loathing; boredom)
6. Surprise: being unprepared for something (amazement; distraction)
7. Trust: a positive emotion (admiration; acceptance)
8. Anticipation: the sense of looking forward positive (vigilance; interest)

Ncbi.nim.nih.gov

Phase 1: Initial or Acute Phase

Postpartum stage 1 is described as the time of rapid change with potential for immediate crises such as postpartum hemorrhage, uterine inversion, amniotic fluid embolisms, and eclampsia. As with post pardon stage 1, everything has changed. With every decision you make, you must make the decision with haste and purpose. One wrong move can cause disaster creating serious complications and trauma. In this phase, as with postpartum, you've got to monitor your blood pressure and stay healthy. There is no time to abuse your body in any form. You do not want to hemorrhage or go into shock from bad decisions you're making with your body and not with your head. Whatever the body does temporarily for a quick fix, the head has the live with the remainder of your days.

Phase 2: Major Change Phase

During postpartum stage 2, the body is undergoing major changes in terms of hemodynamics, genitourinary, recovery, metabolism, and emotional status. Nonetheless, the changes are less rapid than in the acute postpartum phase, and the patient is generally capable of self-identifying problems. These may run the gamut from ordinary concerns about perineal discomfort to severe postpartum depression.

As with postpardon stage 2, guard your heart. Don't offer it to anyone while you are trying to heal. As stated in phase 1, maintaining your blood pressure is vital. Your heart, which is a vital organ where blood flows through cavities, provides a steady supply of oxygen to all tissues and organs of the body (Abiomed.com).

In this stage, with the right help, you can thrive. Identify and don't be afraid to ask for help. Without help, you can and will sink to your lowest low. Your recovery is vital to you returning to a normal state of health, mind, strength. Recovery is the action or process of you regaining possession or control of something stolen or lost (Dictionary.com). There is no one better to find the lost you than yourself.

Time is on your side. You do not have to prove anything to yourself or to anyone else that you can get a spouse. Getting a man or woman is easy. You can take an application, but don't hire. When you get ready to hire, interview, interview, interview.

And of course, do a background check. The position that you are filling is for long-term with benefits. You want to make sure that the next person you hire to be your spouse understands what they are signing up for. Be very clear during the interview of what you offer and what your expectations are for the position. Also, include a probationary period. It's okay to end a relationship if you start seeing red flags. Don't be like the former me ignoring the red, blue, and green flags. And for goodness sake, don't change the probationary period. If the probationary period is three months, stick with it. If it is six months, a year, whatever. It's the same course of action. You are the only one to determine the threshold. If you amend the pro-

106

bationary period even one time, you'll do it again and again until it is nonexistent.

When you view this process as you would as an employer, you'll understand that the best employees do their job because they have clear communication from you, and you provide the benefits and pay increase as scheduled. On the other hand, horrible employees, with lack of communication, do not show up to work, only give seventy percent at best when they do show up and, in some cases, cost you more money in the end for lack of production. You want to very selective in your hiring process. It's time to finally have some productive years in your life!

Phase 3: Restoration Phase

During postpartum stage 3, the time of restoration of muscle tone and connective tissue to the prepregnant state. Although change is subtle during this phase, it behooves caregivers to remember that a woman's body is nonetheless not fully restored to prepregnant physiology until about six months postdelivery. Some changes to the genitourinary system are much longer in resolving, and some may never fully revert to the prepregnant state.

> Restore: bring back into existence, use or the like; reestablish (Dictionary.com)

It is your time to shine. But I won't lie to you. Restoration takes time, and you will be tested. This will be the hardest step and the longest step. Just like postpregnancy, you want your body back now, but it takes time. You want your free time back now, but that takes strategic planning. Although you know you are on the other side of the train wreck you've just experience, fear still finds a cracked window or door to invite itself in. In my case, it got worse before it got better, but it did get better.

Fear is an unpleasant emotion caused by the belief that something is dangerous, likely to cause pain, or a threat. That is exactly what my emotions were during stage one of postpardon. It was unpleasant for me to tell anyone, even my children, that I was getting a divorce again. My youngest son, bless his heart, said to me, "Again, Mom?."

It hurt my feelings, but he didn't mean anything by it. How could he? His fifteen-year-old self knew nothing about affairs of the heart and brokenness. Heck, during the period of my writing this book, I still got creepy late-night texts or DM from "associates," not friends, that I haven't heard from in over a year, asking, "How is Robert Earl?"

I can laugh about it now. I stare at the text of these nosy individuals and say to myself, "Dang, they ain't even asked about me." I know that's bad grammar, but that is how I felt looking at an odd text in the morning from someone who does not give a hoot about my welfare. They're just trying to confirm the gossip they've heard. It has been said that most folks don't care how you're doing. Half are happy that your life is turned upside down, and the other half are just glad it's not them.

Healing

The danger that we feel talking about our experience is not knowing how much pain we will conjure up. That's one of our fears. I've been working on this book since my divorce—more than twenty-four months. It was and still is therapy for me. But it also causes me great pain to relive the most recent divorce as well as divorce 1 and 2. I forgot Warden 1 cheated on me three times until I started writing. You see, even if you forgave the wardens for their past atrocities against you, your heart still sighs because you're disappointed in that particular journey you had with them, what they did, and what you did respectively. *Oh, if I could do it all over again*, you pronounce in your head. Pain can turn into threats quickly if you let it.

I've heard the Honorable Bishop T. D. Jakes say that pain is a lot of information quick. Yes, sir, it is indeed. The threats, verbal and/or physical, can be aimed at yourself or other individuals. You may feel like harming yourself, the person who hurt you or inadvertently hurt the new person who has come into your life. Everyone is suffering because you are hurting. My bishop, Honorable Bishop Ronnie Crudup, says this all the time: hurt people, hurt people.

This is where depression has creeped in. For me, I denied that I was depressed every time. I have always considered myself to be a strong woman, a strong black woman, if you will. In my fifty-three years, there has never been time for a scheduled nervous breakdown, but one was always on the horizon. Although these silent breakdowns occurred, they were never acknowledged or dealt with properly. Instead, I participated in disorderly conduct to cover up what was so painfully existing.

Because depression is a mood disorder, feelings of sadness and loss opens a door for a path of destructive behavior, which can develop at any moment. When you read the words "harm yourself," most individuals immediately think suicide. Unfortunately, some have decided to take that route, an out. I hope that my book helps someone not to end their precious life because of an unfortunate occurrence in their life. There is so much more to look forward to.

But harming oneself comes in many forms. Emotionally, you check out and withdraw yourself from true friends and supportive family because you get tired of the unsolicited counseling and stares of them feeling sorry for you as if their life is so much better.

Physically, you may participate in one of these activities: deny oneself food, overeat, use of excessive alcohol, use drugs, and/or become promiscuous (the practice of engaging in sexual activity frequently with different partners or being indiscriminate in the choice of sexual partners). Yeah, I can honestly say that I've engaged in all these harmful behaviors, except drugs. I'm too scared to go to jail, so not doing drugs has never been a problem for me. I don't care how depressed I get; my mind will not be that far gone where I know I could get a prison sentence for buying illegal drugs.

On the other hand, I have been wasted by legalized liquor to the point where I did not recall the complete route of my driving home. To myself and my boys, I am eternally sorry. At any of those times, I could have harmed myself, leaving my children without a mom, or worse, injuring or killing someone else and leaving their children without a parent.

As the mood disorders continue to unravel you, the anxiety kicks in, and you think you'll never be loved again. Well, you say to yourself, *I'll fix that.* You start buying clothes too tight, too short, and too loose. It's time to prove to the world that you are worth something. After pardoning myself from wardens 1 and 2, I hit the clubs. I needed validation that I was fine, beautiful, and wanted. Seek and you shall find. Not knowing what to do, I just did what everyone else did when my marriage ended.

All this ill activity served no purpose. In the end, I just traded in the one warden for several trustees with my promiscuous behavior. They were wardens in training. Oh, if I could do it all over again. Well I did. I did do it over again when I divorced warden number 3. But this time, instead of thinking I needed to validate myself, I used the other V word—value—and honored myself. I placed value where it was way overdue, not needing to seek any validation from anyone, friend or foe.

Like you, I felt anger, the bitterness, and the resentment. I didn't want to feel this way, but I was on autopilot. In order to give birth to the new me, I was going to need to push out the anger, bitterness, and resentment. Anger can pattern itself in the form of annoyance, displeasure, or hostility. Now, let's be clear. All of the emotions are natural for a human. The difference is the amount of time that you hang on to the anger, bitterness, and resentment. Therein lies the problem(s).

> Be ye angry, and sin not; let not the sun go down
> upon your wrath. (Ephesians 4:26)

> Let all bitterness and wrath and anger and clamor
> and slander be put away from you, along with all
> malice. Be kind to one another, tender-hearted,
> forgiving each other, just as God in Christ also
> has forgiven you. (Ephesians 4:31–32)

Sometimes, as I read the scriptures above, I would just roll my eyes and declare to myself I will keep this anger as long as I want to. That, my friend, was not a good decision. Any of the days I held on to a memory that angered or annoyed me, I would have headaches, and some nights, I would have to wear a mouth guard just to not grind my teeth from the stress of it. My dreams are very action oriented, so even after having eight hours of sleep, I would wake up exhausted from being a ninja and fighting any and everything in my dreams. Who knew that the Bible gave some great advice regarding not letting the sun go down on your wrath? That was me being funny.

For the most part, I realized I was angry with my myself more so than any of the wardens. I had to find a way to forgive me first. That's part of be accountable to God, yourself, and the wardens.

Yeah, I know you're thinking you don't have to forgive or be accountable to those wardens, but you do. You have to sit down and account for your actions and reactions as well as his. In accounting, there are debit columns and credit columns. You have to decide what and where are the debits and credits in your life and settle them up accordingly. If you're not careful with your accounting, you'll end up in overdraft just like your checking account. Watch what you do; watch what you say. At the end of the day, you just want to keep good records so you can stay in the black. Quora.com states that staying in black means that you've earn enough money to pay your expenses. Hilarious! And UrbanDictionary.com defines staying in the black as "take care of yourself." This simply means stays focused so you can plan some fabulous trips, and don't dwell on the past I like to call warden Ville!

Testing 1, 2, 3

All of this is easier said than done. When you make a decision to do better and rid yourself of the bitterness, all hell can break loose. It's a test. During this stage where I was doing my best not to be bitter, the unforeseeable and unimaginable happened. My car stopped on a very busy street at 7:28 a.m. It just stopped—no warning, nothing. All I could think about was that someone is going to rear-end me, my car would catch on fire, and my boys would have no mom.

As I frantically called AAA, a policeman was coming around the corner. He was my angel. He pulled up beside me and said, "Don't cry, pretty lady. I'll park behind you so no one will hit you." My fear tuned into joy momentarily. The AAA rep on the phone advised me that Warden 3 had taken me off the account and that she could still dispatch a driver, but I would have to pay. What purpose did that serve of his taking me off the account? It was already paid for, for the year.

The bitterness swelled back up in me. Those three-, four-, five-letter words started uttering from my lips. I barely had any money. Like most Americans, I was just living paycheck to paycheck. I called a friend, and she said that I could use her AAA account, but the AAA driver could not use her account because she was not in the car with me, but this sweet soul only charged me twenty dollars for the tow—another angel from God. People don't have to be nice to you. When they are, their hearts are touched by God.

The initial diagnosis from the dealership was that the high-pressure fuel pump (HPFP) failed and that it would be fixed at no cost to me because it was under the extended limited warranty that BMW North America had provided. The anxiety left me for a brief moment. I was given a loaner, and all was right with the world. I was breathing normally again and going about my life postpardon.

Three weeks after the dealership held my car for repair, I got a call stating that they've fixed the HPFP, but there is another issue. The timer chain failed, and it was going to cost me twenty-one thousand dollars. Yes, you heard me correctly. I screamed into the phone, "The devil is a lie," and pulled over to the side of the road for fear of hitting someone. My heart was racing, my hands were shaking, and my head was trying to compute what this man was telling me. I told him to explain to me like I was a two-year-old how this barely-four-year-old car that cost almost sixty thousand dollars (paid in full) was now in need of a new engine and why I needed to come up with the twenty-one thousand.

He replied, "Well, BMW North American will give you a discount, making it only seventeen thousand dollars. Welp. Y'all know those three-, four-, five-letter words started shooting out again. Pray for me. God ain't through with me yet. I asked this man in my mother's voice, "Am I to pull seventeen thousand out of my butt?" I did use a more colorful word, of course. He still is not telling me why, just repeating the cost of the repair. I found myself in yet another bitter battle that would last six months. I had just divorced warden number 3 four months prior.

I was almost in a happy place, and this set me right back into despair and bitterness. My car was my bread and butter. I am a realtor, and at that particular time in my life, my marketing dollars for real estate and mad money came from my side hustle as an Uber/Lyft driver. Now, all of that came to a screeching halt.

Although I was worried, I kept telling myself, it would be okay. A Dodge Ram truck had hit me head on the previous year, and I was due a settlement. All I know is ain't no feeling like the feeling you have when you are flat broke and you know there is a large check with your name on it and you can't get to it.

I tried to stay positive during this time, but days turned into weeks and weeks into months. I had spent every nickel I had, charged up all my credit cards, mortgage was past due, and was borrowing money from my grown sons. My pride took a big hit. Each time I borrowed money from my boys, this scripture rang loud in my head of what St. Paul the Apostle said:

> Behold, the third time I am ready to come to you; and I will not be burdensome to you: for I seek not yours, but you: for the children ought not to lay up for the parents, but the parents for the children. (2 Corinthians 12:14)

I know my boys did not find it burdensome to help me out. That was my feeling some type of way because I'm supposed to be the one to lend and give, not them. In a period of eighteen months of my life, it seemed that Murphy's law was whipping my butt. My mom died of cancer, I divorced warden number 3, car catastrophe, loom and gloom over my head regarding income and the threat of losing my home, and then another event that just broke my heart. Warden number1 died.

My two oldest sons' father died of a sudden heart attack a week before Christmas that no one saw coming. I grieved for my friend. I grieved for my boys. I grieved for his mom and sister. No matter what you read in the earlier chapter of this book regarding warden number 1, we had become the best co-parents to our boys and had a great postdivorce relationship for more than twenty-five years. When I purchased my home, he sincerely told me how proud he was for me. He would come over and spend hours in the boys' room, playing video games with them. I would forget he was there. I told him on one occasion I was going to charge him rent. My family and I loved him dearly. He was a great dad. Now my attention turned off of poor me and to my boys. Their father was gone. I knew the ache their hearts would feel because I was still grieving Mama.

Again, God provided angels to supplement my none income. Without asking, a dear friend sent me a very large check in the mail saying it was my Christmas gift. I had enough funds to pay for our room and food for the trip to Arkansas, but I had no money to buy my dear friend a flower for his grave. I was so hard on myself during this time. I could not believe at fifty-one years old, here was I with almost nothing. But I had better than "nothing." My needs were met, not my wants, and that's what was causing me to focus on the negative instead of the positive. That was the perspective in my head. Perspective is defined "as a particular attitude toward or way of regarding something; a point of view" (Oxford Dictionary).

These unimaginable events in your life are tests. After you go through any test, written or mankind, you always look back and say, "That wasn't so bad. Why did I stress so much?"

Or you may say, "That was hard, really hard. Next time, I'll be better prepared."

The Emergency Broadcast System that was initiated in 1963 during the Kennedy administration allowed the president to address the entire nation in an emergency. These announcements still exist today on the first of the month at noon. The recorded message says, "This is a test. For the next sixty seconds, this station will conduct a test of the Emergency Broadcast System. This is only a test." Oh, if our test were only sixty seconds in real life.

I didn't always have this perspective in viewing the test of life that come my way, but I do now. Some events that happen to you are absolute emergencies, while others are only a test and you should respond accordingly.

After I changed my perspective, I was able to handle this action without tears, reservation, or shame. I remember telling a friend that I could not possibly borrow another cent from my boys to buy grocery. She said, "Sharon, go get some food stamps." I had not even thought of that, not because I would be embarrassed like I was as a child. No, I just had not thought of it.

Sure enough, I hitched a ride with my son one morning and went to the local office and applied. I got myself an EBT card. I will remember that day for as long as I live. That place had the same Pine-Sol smell it had back in the '70s, even though it was in a different location. You see, as a child, I was familiar with the welfare office. They call it Department of Human Services now.

I grew up on food stamps. My bougie self hated being on stamps as a kid; it meant we were poor. I, on the other hand, did not believe we were poor. Heck, I didn't even know what poor meant. I just remember some looks we got in the stores when Mama paid for the groceries with the stamps, or someone telling me we were poor because we got stamps. Otherwise, I didn't know any difference outside of Prosperity Street. We all looked the same, and we all lived in the same type of houses in the '70s.

My mom belonged to this group called the Welfare Rights Organization. She took us on many trips with her to the local welfare office. It wasn't until my mom's death, upon research, that I realize the instrumental part my mom had in the "welfare rights" for the citizens of this area. I did not know this was a national organization. I did not know what their true agenda and fight was for. I was a child, and I was in a child's place in the back room while grown folks handled grown folks' business.

This is why this moment at the welfare office was so special to me. God had allowed it. I looked at the faces of the women and children who were there. I said to myself, *My mom used to fight for women like them and me.* It made me smile, and more importantly, it made me proud. I pretended she was sitting next to me in the empty chair and carried on a conversation in my head with her.

Eventually, all my current storms began to cease, I realized I was passing my tests. I did not go back to Pharaoh—aka Warden number 3—when trouble found me. I lay on the floor of my home most days and told God I did not like it—*it* being all the storms—but I was not afraid, and I would not return to Egypt my former life. I reminded myself of all the rescues God had brought me out of before. Why should this season be any less?

My tests were the best thing to happen to me. I know that sounds weird. But during the storms, I got to see what friends and family were truly available to me. I got to spend more time with my oldest son during our rides on days I had to borrow his car. Neither one of us knew that the following year, he and his wife would move back to her home state. That was God giving me that time with my son that I would have otherwise not had. Priceless. I got to spend more time with God, and I got to write this book. I hope that this book has blessed you and that it gives you the courage to keep going, to pardon yourself from every warden, trustee, and ghost in your life. Although this book is written specifically about pardoning yourself from an unhealthy relationship, you can pardon yourself from anything unhealthy in your life. Toxic friends, job, etc. You are great. You are whom God created you to be. I once wrote in my Facebook feed that when we envy someone else's life, we tell God we are not happy with whom He created us to be. Once you realized that He made you and not a second-rate version of someone else, peace will find its place in your soul. You will finally be able to pardon yourself, the person who deserves and needs the pardon the most.

Transparency is teaching.
Transparency is healing.

I pray that singles and married folks who read my story will heed the wisdom of experience: mine, their own, and other individuals that have been placed in your life. I pray that you have prosperous relationships and marriages because you will "do" better and not "try."

ACKNOWLEDGMENTS

Sons

To my beloved sons, Kenneth, James, and Sean. You've lived through what I've lived through, some good and some not so good. It was my God-given duty to protect you from the moment you came from my womb. I know I let you down at times by my misguided decision-making.

There is not a day that goes by that I don't regret some of the things you saw me endure during my marriages. For that, I am truly sorry. I pray that you live each day with a sense of direction and learn from my experiences and that you are not too scarred to enjoy a healthy relationship for the remainder of your days. You are so loved not only by me, but your fathers too. Your DNA is filled with incredible strength, intelligence, and courage. I pray that your days are long, healthy, and happy. With all my love, Mommy!

Girlfriends

If I start naming, I'm going to get in trouble. Besides saying thank you, I want to say I love you. Your calls, hugs, and prayers have been the greatest gifts a girl can have. Thank you for listening to me vent when needed to. I've enjoyed the journey with each one of you. I'll cherish the memories forever!

Bishop Crudup

My dearest Bishop. I am unworthy of your prayers. You have always, always, welcomed this 'prodigal daughter' home when she strayed from the church. You always welcomed me with a smile and a hug. Thank you from the bottom of my heart. I hope I make you proud in the latter days of my life.

Siblings

To the craziest group of siblings on earth. My sisters, Betty Boo (Nene) and Linda Sue; my brothers, Charles, Willie (bug), Bloomfield (boom boom), Donald (Towntaker), and Robert (Redd). I love you all.

Ms. Patsy

Before the world had "influencers", there was you. Thank you for being the best first mentor a twelve-year-old girl could have. The lessons you taught me have and will never vanish from my soul. Thank you for taking me to the James Robinson Crusade and following through to make sure this baby Christian had a good church home.

Carla

From the day I set foot in your office, we clicked. Thank you so much for your guidance in the world of real estate. And thank you especially for your patience and love as I navigated through some of the worst years of my life. There were days I simply felt lost. Your smile and sincere calls meant the world to me.

Mike

My first celebrity boss. What a privilege it was to work for you and with you. You are the coolest dude ever! My 007 buddy for life, thank you for every opportunity you afforded to me and for being a great friend when I needed one. Your thoughtfulness will never be forgotten.

Mother

There is not a day that goes by that I don't miss you. I won't fret too much because I know you are with the Lord. Thank you for every single lesson you taught me. The ones I liked and the ones I did not appreciate until now. Wow, Mama! I wish I had listened. Nonetheless, thank you for showing me how to give to others. I watch you give 100 percent selflessly to everyone you met. I never told you how courageous you were in my eyes. Absolutely fearless. I often thought I could never be like mama! Guess what, I'm getting there. Yes, ma'am. I'm not letting people run over me as I use to. I didn't understand why I could not be as courageous as you were. Now I know. Only life can build a courageous spirit like the one you had. Thank you for it all, Mama!

ABOUT THE AUTHOR

Sharon Moman is a lifelong resident of the great state of Mississippi. She is a realtor who enjoys the happiness and joy given to her clients when they find their dream home. She is, without a doubt, the biggest Cleveland Browns fan on this side of the Mason-Dixon Line. The Browns were her first love at age twelve in 1979.

Her other and true loves are her three sons, Kenneth, James, and Sean—a mama's pride, for whom her life finds God's truest joy!

When not selling homes, Sharon enjoys her new love of writing and of course, reading and searching biblical scriptures. To her, it feels like a treasure hunt. Secrets to unfold are abundant.

Pardon: The Courage to Be Set Free is Sharon's first book but not the last.

CPSIA information can be obtained
at www.ICGtesting.com
Printed in the USA
LVHW090507310721
694023LV00003B/558